LIVE in The LIGHT

~

Believe in the light while you have the light, so that you may become children of light."
John 12:36 (NIV)

~

A study of Jesus through
Matthew, Mark, Luke, John and beyond.
Your word is a lamp for my feet, a light on my path.
Psalm 119:105 (NIV)

Book 2 of 4 in the L.I.G.H.T. series

(L.ife I.n G.od H.olds T.ruth) (John 8:12)

#1 TRUST in The LIGHT (John 12:46)
#2 LIVE in The LIGHT (John 12:36)
#3 REST in The LIGHT (1 John 1:7)
#4 VICTORY in The LIGHT (John 1:5)

JANETTE KIEFFER

Redeeming Grace 99|1 Ministries
1001-A E. Harmony Rd.
#46
Fort Collins, Colorado 80525

TO THE WAY, THE TRUTH AND THE LIFE
(JOHN 14:6)

To him who is able to keep you from stumbling and to present you before his glorious presence without fault and with great joy - to the only God our Savior be glory, majesty, power and authority, through Jesus Christ our Lord, before all ages, now and forevermore! Amen. Jude 1:24-25 (NIV)

...and to Mark and Mary Ellen Sidler

(My dad and mom.) I love you so very much. You've shown me how to squeeze every drop of joy out of life and to look up and see the sun rise on each fresh new day He gifts us.
You always have, and continue to show me how to truly LIVE in The LIGHT.

Those who are wise will shine like the brightness of the heavens, and those who lead many to righteousness, like the stars for ever and ever. Daniel 12:3 (NIV)

CONTENTS

WELCOME

Greetings dear one,

Thank you for meeting me here. I have been praying for you and no doubt have you come to hold this study in your hands but by sheer answered prayer. Prayer that what is written here would honor Him in every way and be an encouragement to His people.

This is book two in a four book study series on the life of Jesus. If you have not had a chance to begin from the beginning that is completely fine, you are welcome to jump in with both feet right here, right now! However I would encourage you to find book one, "TRUST in The Light" at some point, if God so leads you, in order to complete this studied portrait of His life story. If you did join us on the journey through book one, "TRUST in The LIGHT" this book number two, "LIVE in The Light" will quite literally pick right up where we left off!

This study will continue to have us dancing to the harmony of the four gospels[1] (Matthew, Mark, Luke and John) and leaping into various other books of the Bible as well because as I'm sure you have heard, the Bible really is the best commentary on itself!

As we seek to intimately know our Savior's heart through an in-depth study of His Word we will twist and turn the looking glass up into His Light for it is only in His Light that we truly see Light (Psalm 36:9). We will look at the questions and situations others in Scripture posed to Jesus and how each afforded Him another opportunity to reveal more of Who He is and wanted to be to them. In turn might we begin to see our questions, trials, setbacks, failures, triumphs and successes all as opportunities for Him to reveal more of His heart to us!

I am praying as we climb this mountain of discovery together taking on one "rock" at time we will at the end be able to look back and see that all those stones have become our stepping stones of remembrance; our Ebenezer's, each one declaring His praise that *"Thus far the LORD has helped us."* (1 Samuel 7:12 NIV) He is faithful!

With a trusting faith emboldened, minds captivated, and hearts enraptured by The King of kings may we never stop climbing our mountain one step at a time! To His praise and glory, when we reach the top (and you will) may you find that all those stones have added up to one giant mountain - conquered… because He said, *"Never will I leave you; never will I forsake you."* (Hebrews 13:5 NIV) … remember beloved, how thus far I have always helped you.

Remember your Ebenezer and keep climbing,
someone needs the Hope you have.

---

[1] NLT Parallel Study Bible © 2011 by Tyndale House Publishers, Inc., Carol Stream, IL 60188. All rights reserved. Pg. 1727-1731 (Harmony of the gospels list referenced.)

STUDY NOTE on "A Time to Reflect" pages:

At the end of each week a space is created for you to just sit at His feet and abide in His heart as He pieces together all that He speaks to you through your week of study with Him. Allow Him to practically apply it to your life in a tangible life changing way as only He could. I am praying He tailor fit His Word to your heart and mind so that the result is beautiful life transformation into more of who He created you to be as a reflection of His Son.

I would also encourage you to consider who God has placed in your sphere of influence that He may have you share what you are learning. The "recipe" you use to share can be aligned to your gifts, abilities and enjoyments. Do you like to take walks? If so, maybe consider using a walk as your "recipe for reflection" with another. Do you like to drink tea or fix cars, bake or plant flowers?! Use what you have where you are at. Do not miss an opportunity to intentionally create a space that you can naturally invite another into.

Follow God's lead as He opens doors for you to share your learnings week to week from His Word. Pray for His wisdom and discernment before even beginning this study that God would go ahead of you to prepare your heart to receive His Word and to fully equip you. Trust Him to provide "recipe of reflection" ideas and opportunities that will honor Him and encourage others - including you!

You shall teach them diligently to your children, and shall talk of them when you sit in your house, and when you walk by the way, and when you lie down, and when you rise. Deuteronomy 6:7 (ESV) Do this so that your children who have not known these instructions will hear them and all learn to fear the LORD your God. Do this as long as you live... (Deuteronomy 31:31 NLT)

Let this be written for a future generation, that a people not yet created may praise the LORD: Psalm 102:18 (NIV)

May grace, peace and living hope be yours in abundance~ Janette

P.S. If you happen to embark on this study with a group of people, there is a blank page at the end of the book which should allow you room to take notes or jot down encouragements, prayers and insights gained within weekly group gatherings. Meeting regularly to discuss and share collectively how God has been moving within each heart as you have met with Him individually during the week is a great way to encourage one another in the faith. Romans 1:12 (NIV) *that is, that you and I may be mutually encouraged by each other's faith.*

WEEK 1

nor will they say, 'See here!' or 'See there!' For indeed, the kingdom of God is within you."
Luke 17:21 (NKJV)

Day 1: Application

Welcome to week one! (Or if you have been traveling through since the beginning of book one, "Trust in The Light", then this may feel more like week eleven!) Either way I know only by God's amazing grace have either of us found each other on this same page so may He receive all glory, honor and praise as we venture forth under His Almighty leadership.

My family was just talking around our lunch table as we all gazed outside at our backyard lawn (which leaves something to be desired with its bare patches, but with 6 kids, a giant dog and a slippy slide it doesn't get much chance to grow). However underneath our bird feeder is another story! The birds kick out so much seed which has produced the most luscious spot of green our yard has ever seen! The kids are thinking we should just use bird seed to help our lawns bare patches since the bird seed seems to be oh so much more effective than regular lawn fertilizer!

Let's pray that God breathe His breath within us, awakening His Holy Spirit to till the soil of our hearts to receive His Word in such a way that it takes deep root, enabling us to receive understanding and insight far beyond ourselves.

Please read Romans 8:31-39 (NIV) and then respond to the five questions given us in verses 31, 32, 33, 34, 35 according to the Scripture.

If God is for us, who can be against us?

He who did not spare his own Son, but gave him up for us all - how will he not also, along with him, graciously give us all things?

_____

Who will bring any charge against those whom God has chosen?

_____

It is God who justifies. Who then is the one who condemns?

_____

Who shall separate us from the love of Christ?

_____

What, then, shall we say in response to these things?

_____

_____

_____

_____

It is possible to know these answers yet not live like we believe them. If you have chosen to believe in Jesus as your Savior, you are in His Family and nothing, nothing can separate you from His love. I pray that you more than just know this Truth but that it so takes root in your heart, that it becomes your filter for all that would come your way via this world. May every situation be strained through this Truth that nothing is stronger in your life than His love for you.

Let His Truth filter reveal His whisper to be deafening even amidst the chaos of this world's distracting lies.

In the study book, "Trust in The Light" we began our journey at the birth of Jesus. Today we come to the point in our journey that will begin our study of the way Jesus LIVED out much of His time here on earth. We will look at how He was able to thrive in a time that was anything but easy and comfortable. We will study how Jesus continued to walk forward in Heavens purpose so that we too might find encouragement through His Word and example to walk forward in faith to the end goal He has purposed in Heaven for each one of us.

Thank you for joining me on this quest for more of our Savior to invade more of us. I'm praying for you. Please record below one thing that God has impacted your heart with as you have begun your study of His life through His Word today. As you close, ask Him to strengthen your resolve to put Him first in your life turning the next ten weeks of study into a life long habit of pursuing His heart truly, madly and deeply.

_____

_____

_____

_____

Beloved of God, thank you muchly~

Day 2: Application is Fertilization

Hi! I'm so excited to get started today, thank you for coming! This study dances to the harmony of the four gospels so as we begin today we will look at a parable recorded in three of the four books. We will be commenting from Matthew for the majority of the day so if you have time for just one of the three readings go ahead and read from the perspective recorded in Matthew. Each day six and seven of the week will afford you time to abide at the feet of Jesus in reflection of your weeks study. You may have time during those days to circle back around to certain segments of Scripture or study that you may not have had time to complete during the week.

Please begin in prayer that God would lead us through His Word today and then savor the following Scriptures. Please meet me on the other side of Matthew 13:1-23 _____, Mark 4:1-20 _____, Luke 8:4-15. _____

In these Scripture passages this week we will notice Jesus teaching via parables which are stories that usually hold an analogy between real life and a spiritual truth.

Matthew 13:10 gives us a question asked by Jesus' disciples, what was it?

_____

Matthew 7:6 warns us about giving to dogs what is sacred or our pearls to pigs. We should never stop sharing the Good News with unbelievers but be wise in your approach as we do not have time to waste. Record what Matthew 10:14 tells us below.

_____

_____

In the next verse (Matthew 13:11) it would seem Jesus is using parables to reveal the secrets of the Kingdom. The Good News of the Kingdom would have been very upsetting to the Roman government at the time, so to speak in parables would have protected His ministry. It also fulfilled Scripture (Jesus was always doing that - fulfilling Scripture!!) What does Isaiah 6:9-10 state? You can paraphrase below.

_____

_____

Jesus wanted everyone to listen and understand. Matthew 13:9 (NIV) tells us, *Whoever has ears, let them hear."* (verse 12) *Whoever has will be given more, and they will have an abundance. Whoever does not have, even what at they have will be taken from them.*

I don't know if you have had the opportunity to teach a class to young people (or adult people) but inevitably you can have the same group of students with the same enthusiastic teacher and you will always have the students who will listen and pay attention to the lesson and soak up every detail alongside those students that goof around and choose to fidget and fuss and focus on anything but the lesson. All students took the same class and had the same opportunity to learn but the desire in the focused students heart to understand and retain will make all the difference in the world when it comes time to perform on a test!

This illustration helped me and makes me think it's the same with the parable teachings of Jesus. Even the inner circle of disciples sometimes had trouble understanding God's meaning but they continued to walk with Him, and they asked Him questions (Matthew 13:36). Don't harden your heart to God's message. Those that earnestly seek Him will find Him. Seek Him now, choose Him now while you have the chance. Please read John 12:40-46 _____ and 2 Peter 3:9-10. _____

Jeremiah 29:13 (NIV) *You will seek me and find me when you seek me with all your heart.*

Does it move your heart like it does mine that Jesus knew ahead of time that not everyone would receive His message or even try to, yet He came down to us - anyway, He followed through on the Father's will to die in our place - anyway!! Have you ever found yourself in a position that asked you to act "anyway"?

_____

_____

If you stepped forward in that act (anyway) how did you feel afterwards?

_____

_____

Matthew 13:11 talks about the secrets of the Kingdom of Heaven which is really that the Kingdom is accessible through salvation in Jesus, the fulfillment of all the Old Testament promises.

Matthew 13:16 (NLT) *But blessed are your eyes, because they see; and your ears, because they hear.* I pray for this over myself and my children. That not only would I perceive Him but then also step out in wholehearted obedience to Him. Jeremiah 5:20-25 _____ issues a warning to all of us. (If it helps keep track of what you have read, go ahead and check the blanks following the Scripture readings.)

The question for Jesus on why He taught in parables reveals His heart for the urgency and authenticity of His mission. He was in the game to play not just to take pictures that would make Him look good. He was searching for sincere worshipers and seekers to cultivate the mission of His heart that the Scriptures all pointed to.

In this parable of the farmer scattering seed what are the four outcomes of each seed? The seed being the Good News.

1. _____

_____

2. _____

_____

3. _____
_____

4. _____
_____

1.) Footpath - birds ate up the good seed. What might be a "bird" in your life that threatens to steal your Truth?

_____

If you feel the threat of vultures overhead cry out to Him like the father in Mark 9:24 (NIV) … *"I do believe; help me overcome my unbelief!"*

2.) Shallow soil - it seems it was not the trial of scorching hot sun that killed the seed, it was that when the trial came they had a root problem. Like a gentle rain on a roof with holes. It wasn't the rain as much as the ill equipped roof that would ruin the inside of the home. What might be preventing your roots from going deeper?

_____

If we are not rooted firmly to Truth even the gentlest of rains will wash us away. If you feel shaky remember 2 Timothy 2:19 (NIV) *Nevertheless, God's solid foundation stands firm, sealed with this inscription: "The Lord knows those who are his," and, "Everyone who confesses the name of the Lord must turn away from wickedness."*

3.) Thorny soil - choked by the thorns it doesn't say the plant died but that it produced no fruit. Could the weight of a trial so full of thorns make it feel as though you have been left for dead but in fact you are not, and find yourself caught just merely existing

_____

Read John 10:10 _____ and Micah 7:8. _____

Paul in 2 Corinthians 12:8-9 experienced his own thorns to which he prayed to God three times asking Him to take it away but what was God's answer according to verse 9? And what was Paul's response?

_____

_____

It would seem Jesus too had to face quite a thorn, actually a crown of thorns (John 19:2) and then being impaled to a cross for OUR sin (Col. 2:14). He too asked His Heavenly Father three times for any other way to accomplish His mission but each time the answer was "no" and what was Jesus' response? See Matthew 26:39-46 _____

_____

John 14:6 tells us Jesus is the ONLY Way to the Father. If there had been another way I'm sure it would have been implemented during these intense moments of prayer between Jesus and the Father. Jesus received a "no" that resulted in an ultimate "yes" for us to receive eternal life. Aren't we all glad He submitted to the Father's will?!!! May we learn from Jesus and trust that our Heavenly Father only says "no" when there is a greater "yes".

4.) Fertile soil - best case scenario! Root down fruit up! If you still have a breath in your lungs and a beat in your heart He still has GREAT purpose for your life that He has promised to bring to completion in His time (Phil. 1:6, Ecc. 3:11).

The production of a harvest takes great patience.

Bowing to His wisdom and authority affords time for Him to grow a patience in us that will be needed to see things from His perspective, to take up peace on the path. Bowing affords time for Him to grow in us a steadfast patient endurance needed as we wait for His promised return. Let us bow to His tender care that through our lives He might produce a mighty harvest to His glory and praise!

Please record the point that has impacted your heart the most from today's study in His Word.

_____

_____

_____

_____

Thank you sincerely.

Day 3: Trusting in The Light

Hello my friend. I'm so very glad you have found your way back to this page amidst all the distractions of this loud world. Thank you for tuning into the whisper in your heart from God Almighty that you are wanted, loved, desired and most invited to abide in His presence right now. Please begin with Him in prayer that He alone take the lead in our study today as we ask that He enable us to follow His Light in obedience, receptive to His tailored Word to our hearts.

Please read Mark 4:21-25 _____ and Luke 8:16-18. _____

Our lives as believers hold the treasure of His Kingdom within and as a light in a lighthouse shines the way to shore, we, like the moon, are to reflect the Son's guiding Light to our Kingdom Home. Our lives rooted firmly in His

Truth will produce a fruitful harvest for Him! In Luke 8:16-17 what is indicated as the best place for a lighted lamp?

_____

On a stand to give light to all! Matthew 5:16 tells us to let our light shine to bring glory to the Father!

God knows the condition of each heart. May He find our's sincerely seeking after His Light. A sincere seeker is an applicator, a doer not just a hearer of His Word. Luke 8:18 (NLT) states, *"So pay attention to how you hear. To those who listen to my teaching, more understanding will be given. But for those who are not listening, even what they think they understand will be taken away from them."* (underlining mine.)

How do you hear?
Do you listen or do you already think you know?
You can't apply God's Word if you haven't truly heard it and application is fertilizer for a strong faith. It's like physical training - at my age it is very apparent if you don't use it you lose it! You can't stand still in faith. You are either growing stronger or growing weaker.

2 Timothy 4:3 (NIV) issues us all a warning, *For the time will come when people will not put up with sound doctrine. Instead, to suit their own desires, they will gather around them a great number of teachers to say what their itching ears want to hear.*

May we be sincere listeners and seekers not of what we think we want to hear but to what He is actually saying and then move on the ground beneath our feet and be applicators of His Word. His powerful and effective Word.

Please record the impact to your heart regarding the power of His Word from the following Scriptures. Isaiah 55:10-12 _____, Hebrews 4:12 _____

_____

_____

_____

Let us take a glance at a beautiful picture of what happens to seed when we entrust it to the Light of His faithful Truth. Please meet me after you have enjoyed Mark 4:26-29. _____

Please fill in the blanks according to the NIV of Mark 4:27.
Night and day, whether he sleeps or gets up, the seed sprouts and grows, though ____
_____ _____ _____ _____.

"He does not know how." Oh praise the Lord with me on that one!!! God is able to bring about a harvest from our labor in Him even when we see absolutely no way and have no idea how. HE IS just ABLE. No need to know how, just WHO dear one!

Who do you allow to cultivate your hearts desires, longings, motives? Do you pray for Him to stir you up with good ideas that will delight His heart? Do you ask for the energy and will to participate? What does James 4:2 tell us about not asking God?

_____

_____

He is able. Delight yourself in the Light of His sustaining Truth and just see what begins to delight your heart!

- ◆ Philippians 2:13 (NIV) *for it is God who works in you to will and to act in order to fulfill his good purpose.* Praise Him for being the Source of all provision for His purpose!

- Colossians 1:29 (NIV) states, *To this end I strenuously contend with all the energy Christ so powerfully works in me.* And praise Him for the supply of energy… the energy to continue to rely on Him for more of His energy each step/breath of the way.

We don't have to know "how", just continue to show up, available to Him and He will be the ability in your availABILITY.

Thank you muchly my friend for digging in with me today. Please record how God impacted your heart the most through your time in His Word today.

_____

_____

_____

_____

Day 4: The Kingdom

Oh, dear one I do believe you have grown overnight in all the most beautiful ways as you have lived trusting in His ability at work in you! Please bow with me in prayer that God Almighty would lead us this day into greater depths of His Truth than we have experienced before!

Please meet me on the other side of Matthew 13:31-32 _____, Mark 4:30-32 _____, and Luke 13:18-19. _____

In two of these passages it records Jesus almost thinking to Himself, asking… How can I describe the Kingdom of God? How can I illustrate it? When was the last time you gave good thought to the Kingdom of God living within your body, His Temple (1 Cor. 6:19)? When was the last time you contemplated how you might intentionally illustrate that fact to the outside world looking in? In thought, word and action how do you illustrate the God within you?

_____

_____

_____

What does Jesus liken the Kingdom to, of all things?!

_____

A mustard seed!!! The smallest of seeds! Jesus came to earth as a humble baby born in a manger - Immanuel... remember back to the beginning of our study in "TRUST in The Light"?! Pretty small and humble beginning by the world's standards. But in this passage what does that little seed do and become?

_____

It thrives! It starts small but has exponential growth!! That seed roots deep and fruits up so much so that birds are able to take refuge within its branches! All who believe in Jesus will take refuge eternally in His overcoming Kingdom! Please look up Zechariah 4:10._____

This tells us not to what?

_____

Do not despise small beginnings!!
Why?

_____

Because God delights to see the work begin!

If not to delight His heart, what are we beginning anything for?!

2 Chronicles 16:9 tells us the eyes of the Lord roam the earth to strengthen what kind of hearts?

_____

Those fully devoted to Him!

Is there anything in your life that seems so small and insignificant? You wonder if it's effective at all?

_____

_____

Are you willing to let God lead and be the judge? To let God be what defines your success rather than the world? Please read Romans 12:2 _____, Hebrews 12:2 _____, and 1 Corinthians 4:5 _____.

He has made everything beautiful in its time. He has also set eternity in the human heart; yet no one can fathom what God has done from beginning to end. Ecclesiastes 3:11 (NIV)

God only creates beautiful things. Do not give up before you see the purpose of your cocoon dear one.

Coast on by Matthew 13:33 _____, and Luke 13:20-21 _____.

How do these verses encourage you?

_____

_____

Yeast is so tiny but it goes a LONG way. It permeates an entire batch of dough making it rise! Please recall the impact you recorded Isaiah 55:11 having earlier on you within yesterdays study. Please write out this verse below.

_____

_____

If you carry the Word which is Jesus Himself (John 1:1-5) within you His Light will cast a glow into this dark world naturally though you and your life will create contrast. A contrast this world desperately craves and so often knows nothing about! LIVE to magnify Truth!

Do not become discouraged because your physical eyes may have yet to align with your spiritual vision. 1 Corinthians 15:58 (NLT) *So, my dear brothers and sisters, be strong and immovable. Always work enthusiastically for the Lord, for you know that nothing you do for the Lord is ever useless.*

Let's roll on to Matthew 13:34-35 _____, and Mark 4:33-34. _____

Our passage in Mark tells us He taught as much as the people could understand! WOW! Can you imagine if we could just handle more how much He could teach us?!! I often pray Job 32:8 for myself as it states that it is the breath of the Almighty that gives one understanding! Oh Lord breathe in me, please!!

As we go out this week may we be a vessel of His Kingdom calling on the One who beckons us in Jeremiah 33:3 (NIV) *'Call to me and I will answer you and tell you great and unsearchable things you do not know.'* May He ignite our hearts with the Light of His Truth that will embolden our faith and increase our trust that the fire He declares His Word to be in Jeremiah 23:29 would become uncontainable as we walk forward in bold faith allowing Him to fulfill the GREAT purpose He started within each one of us!

Please record the greatest point of impact made to your heart today.

_____

_____

_____

_____

But if I say, "I will not mention his word or speak anymore in his name," his word is in my heart like a fire, a fire shut up in my bones. I am weary of holding it in; indeed I cannot. Jeremiah 20:9 (NIV)

Day 5: Personal Relationship

You have made it to the end of week one! I commend your tenacity and diligence to have made an effort to prioritize time with your Creator God. In a world that can be so busy, demanding and distracting you have allowed God's strength and voice calling you, pursuing your heart, to take precedence. Well done!

Please bow in prayer before preceding, thanking Him for stirring up within us a craving for more of Him in our hearts as we ask that He continue to draw us deeper into His illuminating Truth.

Please glance back at Matthew 13:34-35 and Mark 4:33-34 as a refresher from yesterday's study.

At what time did Jesus explain the parables to His disciples?

_____

When they were ALONE together! Does this speak to the importance of your own quiet alone time with the Lord?

This rendition in the book of Matthew points to the Old Testament. Please see Psalm 78:2 compared to Matthew 13:35.

It is so very important for us to be passing down the timeless Truth of our Savior to our children, to those of the next generation.

1 Corinthians 2:7 (NIV) *No, we declare God's wisdom, a mystery that has been hidden and that God destined for our glory before time began.* His plan for us was made before the world even began!! Hallelujah! Our God is never without a plan or purpose for your life even when we feel it is all a big mystery. Be patient and trust as He works out to completion that which He has started! (See Philippians 1:6)

Please read Romans 16:25-27 _____.
Why has this plan been revealed? (verse 26)

_____

So that we might believe, obey and be saved!

What insight does 1 Peter 1:8-12 give us?

_____

Our salvation is GREAT!

How often do we wake up and fit our head with the helmet of salvation (Eph. 6:17)? Are we guarding our mind and fixing our thoughts on things above and not earthly things with eagerness (Col. 3:2)?

Even when we forget our spiritual helmet in the morning it's never too late to pray it on... Psalm 51:12 (NIV) *Restore to me the joy of your salvation and grant me a willing spirit, to sustain me.*

Please visit Matthew 13:24-30, and verses 36-43. _____

According to verses 36-43 explain this parable as you understand it.
   ◆   Who is the farmer?

_____

The Son of Man, the One that came to be the bridge to God the Father.
   ◆   What is the field?

_____

The world.
   ◆   What is the good seed?

_____

The people of the Kingdom.

- What are the weeds?

_____

Those that belong to the evil one.

- Who planted the weeds among the wheat?

_____

The devil. So truly our struggle is not against flesh and blood but against the spiritual forces of evil (Eph. 6:12). Good thing we have the overcoming positive force of Him who is in us, stronger than the enemy of this world (1 John 4:4)!!

- The harvest is what and who are the harvesters?

_____

The end of the world and the angels sent by God will harvest the world.

We must remember only God is qualified to make judgment on people. When we do so we run the risk of damaging some of the good "plants" or people. Let's judge ourselves rather than analyze others. Let us spend more time making sure our own faith is fertilized into application rather than analyzing another application of their fertilization.

Romans 1:20 (NIV) *For since the creation of the world God's invisible qualities--his eternal power and divine nature--have been clearly seen, being understood from what has been made, so that people are without excuse.* Romans 1:31 tells us some will refuse to understand, let that not be us! Romans 2:13-14 (NLT) *For merely listening to the law doesn't make us right with God. It is obeying the law that makes us right in his sight. Even Gentiles, who do not have God's written law, show that they know his law when they instinctively obey it, even without having heard it.*

I've heard it stated that it is not about knowing more but rather doing more with what you know. The doing will come about naturally as we stay connected to the Vine, the source of Truth. See John 15:5.

What does Jeremiah 31:31-34 tell us about the new covenant?

_____

_____

May our own response to God be continually authenticated by a sincere relationship with Him. So often it is our actions that speak louder to others than our words.

What picture does Matthew 13:43 paint for us?

_____

And how does that compare to Daniel 12:3?

_____

The righteous in Jesus will shine like the stars!! Oh glorious day! Truly we must prepare our hearts and our minds to remain steadfast in Him because one day, one day dear one, He is just going to blow our ever lovin' minds with His glorious return!!

My Father's house has many rooms; if that were not so, would I have told you that I am going there to prepare a place for you? And if I go and prepare a place for you, I will come back and take you to be with me that you also may be where I am. You know the way to the place where I am going." John 14:2-4 (NIV)

John 14:6 (NIV) Jesus answered, "I am the way and the truth and the life....

God has prepared the Way, He is preparing a place, what are we doing to prepare to enter? Just believe. Trust and obey as you prepare to be amazed!! If you have never prayed to accept God as your personal Savior, today, right now is the time! None of us is guaranteed another moment in life. Right now is a gift. May we choose to use it receiving His free gift of eternal life in prayer.

There is no one magic prayer just a personal decision to believe between you and God. Such as...

Dear Heavenly Father, I know that I am a sinner in need of a Savior and I believe Jesus, that You are it. I believe in your sacrifice on the cross in my place for the forgiveness of sin. I believe You died and rose again and are the victorious One and only Truly God, the only way to Heaven. I give my life to You. Please come into my heart and live forever. In Jesus name I pray, Amen.

If you prayed to receive Jesus as your Savior for the first time welcome to the family of God dear one!! I encourage you to tell another believer that will be able to celebrate your new life in Christ and encourage you on your journey.

Luke 15:7 (NIV) *I tell you that in the same way there will be more rejoicing in heaven over one sinner who repents than over ninety-nine righteous persons who do not need to repent.*

Please take a moment before wrapping up this week of study to pause in review of some of the points we have covered this week. Record what has impacted you the most from your time with God today below.

- God uses small things for GREAT big impact
- Do not despise small beginnings
- We don't have to know "how" when we can just trust He is able
- In Him we can always choose the joy of His salvation

_____

_____

_____

_____

God bless you muchly~

Day 6 & 7: At His Feet - A Time to Reflect

Over the next two days take time to reflect over your week of study. Maybe you need some time to catch up on the study material and this might be the perfect break to do just that with the Lord!

I encourage you to glance back at the final point at the end of each day that you recorded having had the greatest impact on your heart. As you spend time with God in prayer, reflect and record on the lines below how God is tying it all together and applying it to your life.

Ask that God make it clear who He would have you invite into a natural opportunity to share Him, to apply what you are learning. Trust Him to continue to take the lead. May we have a heart ever ready with eyes and ears out to the opportunities God wants to invite us into for His glory and praise.

Do not merely listen to the word, and so deceive yourselves. Do what it says. Anyone who listens to the word but does not do what it says is like someone who looks at his face in a mirror and, after looking at himself, goes away and immediately forgets what he looks like. But whoever looks intently into the perfect law that gives freedom, and continues in it - not forgetting what they have heard, but doing it - they will be blessed in what they do. James 1:22-25 (NIV)

_____

_____

_____

_____

_____

Philippians 4:13 (NIV) *I can do all things through him who gives me strength.* John 14:26 (NIV) *But the Advocate, the Holy Spirit, whom the Father will send in my name, will teach you all things and will remind you of everything I have said to you.*

WEEK 2

Though you have not seen him, you love him; and even though you do not see him now, you believe in him and are filled with an inexpressible and glorious joy, 1 Peter 1:8 (NIV)

Day 1: LIVE Enamored

Hi! Have you heard the saying, you are not really rich until you have something that money can't buy!? Do you have something like that? Today we will study Scripture that proves we ALL have something like that! Praise the Lord!

Before we begin please bow with me in prayer, thanking our Lord for all that He is and wants to be to us. May He awaken our souls to a deeper craving for more of Him. *Let the morning bring me word of your unfailing love, for I have put my trust in you. Show me the way I should go, for to you I entrust my life. Psalm 143:8 (NIV)*

We are going to begin in Matthew chapter 13. Please read verse 44. _____

What emotional state is the man in who finds this treasure?

_____

Joyful - excited!

In his joy what is he doing?

_____

Selling all he has?! What?! And he is filled with JOY?!!

What would be worth so much that selling ALL you had would bring you great joy to own it?

_____

The Kingdom of Heaven exceeds the value of ALL other treasures. What do the following verses indicate the value of the Kingdom to be worth?

Matthew 19:21

Sell EVERYTHING, give it to the poor and you will have treasure in heaven.

Matthew 19:29

Give up EVERYTHING to receive 100 times in return AND eternal life.

Philippians 3:7

What we once thought had value becomes awash in comparison to the value of truly knowing Jesus.

This man in Matthew 13:44 discovered what was hidden and was able to recognize its incredible value. It cost everything he had yet he paid nothing for the gift itself. How would you describe this Truth?

The cost is submitting to His Higher will and purpose for your life… in EVERYTHING. But that cost pales in comparison to the gift of eternal life that cost our God EVERYTHING to make it not only available but also FREE to us who would choose to believe.

Like this man, do we realize the sheer value of the treasure we have in Him? Do we realize it to the point we are willing to surrender our families, friends, workplaces, finances, health and say, "Not my will, but Yours be done." just as Jesus did in the Garden of Gethsemane just before He was taken to the cross?

We can always pray that He stir up that desire in us or re-stir again and again each time we feel ourselves settling back into me-myself-and I mode.

Philippians 3:10-11 (NIV) *I want to know Christ - yes, to know the power of his resurrection and participation in his sufferings, becoming like him in his death, and so, somehow, attaining to the resurrection from the dead.*

Please read Matthew 13:45-46. _____

In this passage the Kingdom is compared to what in contrast to our last passage of study?

_____

Here the Kingdom is compared to the merchant where the Kingdom was last compared to the treasure, found by the man.

Here Jesus is showing us another aspect of the Kingdom. The treasure found in this passage is symbolic of what?

_____

We are the pearl of great treasure! The King was willing to pay the price for us! We meant so much to Him that He was willing to pay the ultimate price we never could have, to redeem us! Do you see yourself as a treasure? God certainly does.

The world often defines worth in accomplishments and appearances but that is not how God defines worth. Take a moment and read Psalm 139 slowly savoring God's love note to you.

He loves you so much He can complete your sentences, He knows what makes your heart smile, and He's thinking of you all the time, He has all your days in

His mighty, capable, equipping hand. Every detail about your personality and appearance was knit together! Knitting is detailed work!! Have you ever seen a ladybug with sloppy spots?! Me neither! He is a detailed God and you matter to Him! You are His priceless treasure.

1 Corinthians 6:20 (ESV) *for you were bought with a price. So glorify God in your body.* Later in our study we will comb the Scriptures detailing the price however our finite minds cannot possibly truly comprehend it.

What are some ways you could glorify God in your body? Please read Colossians 3:17 before answering.

_____

_____

Let's skip over now to Matthew 13:47-52. _____

In this parable what is the Kingdom compared to?

_____

A fishing net! What does Jesus tell His disciples in Matthew 4:19?

_____

The NIV phrases it, "I will send you out to fish for people." I will send you... I will... The one who sends out a group of explorers on safari makes sure the group is well equipped with all they will need to ensure the greatest success. It is the guide, the one who does the sending out that knows best what the group will need. They have been that way before, they know the terrain, they are the experts and the group would do well to take their advice, their equipping, and follow it if they don't want to get eaten by the prey!

What direction has God given us on our safari, our mission?

Therefore go and make disciples of all nations, baptizing them in the name of the Father and of the Son and of the Holy Spirit, and teaching them to obey everything I have commanded you. And surely I am with you always, to the very end of the age." Matthew 28:19-20 (NIV)

We do not get to determine who gets in the Kingdom and who does not. That judging is left to One infinitely more qualified than any human. We are just to take the net, the Kingdom, that is within us, the precious saving knowledge of Jesus Christ, to all the world, starting at, and on, the ground beneath our own two feet.

Matthew 13:49 speaks of the end of the world and then in verse 51 it asks if we understand. Do you also sense the urgency to make the decision to live for Christ, to know and share the Truth before it's too late?! None of us are guaranteed the next moment, the time is now!

In closing please read 1 Peter 1:3-9. _____

Verse 8-9 (NLT) *You love him even though you have never seen him. Though you do not see him now, you trust him; and you rejoice with a glorious, inexpressible joy. The reward for trusting him will be the salvation of your souls.*

Go LIVE enamored with the Truth!!

Please record what made the greatest impact on your heart today.

_____

_____

_____

_____

Day 2: Crossing To The Other Side

Hello dear one. I'm so glad you are back today. Does today's title make anyone else a bit apprehensive? Crossing to the other side of what, how, when, why and with who Lord?!! Anyone else relate to me?! I am praying as we embark on our study today, that His name be honored throughout our time and that we are encouraged through His faithful Word. Romans 1:12 (NLT) *When we get together, I want to encourage you in your faith, but I also want to be encouraged by yours.*

Go ahead and dive into our comparative passages for today in Matthew 8:23-27, _____ and Mark 4:35-41, _____ and Luke 8:22-25. _____

Here is a treasured, life preserving verse to tuck into your heart's pocket today: *For God has not given us a spirit of fear, but of power and of love and of a sound mind. 2 Timothy 1:7 (NKJV)*

Mark 4:35 (NLT) records Jesus saying what? "Let's _____ to the _____ _____ __ ___ _____."
(Let's cross to the other side of the lake.)

When Jesus sets a destination you can be sure you will make it. Philippians 1:6 tells us what He starts He finishes. Praise Him!

Jesus tells them this BEFORE they even embark on the journey. How often do we forget in the middle of our storm His promises that He has so faithfully proven to us in our past to be trustworthy?!

This verse 35 also depicts that evening had come. I don't know about you but evening is not my best time to be doing any heavy lifting with my brain! I've lived long enough to know to sit on any big decisions until the morning. Things always seem a bit brighter in the morning!

Look up Lamentations 3:22-23 and record why we are not consumed? Record also what these verses have to say about what we can receive new each and every morning because of His faithfulness.

_____

_____

So as we are weathering the evening hours or any other storm filled hour, we can cling to His precious promises as our life preserver. Such promises as, Psalm 4:8 (NIV) I*n peace I will lie down and sleep, for you alone, LORD, make me dwell in safety.* And Isaiah 26:3 (NIV) *You will keep in perfect peace those whose minds are steadfast, because they trust in you.*

The disciples followed Jesus into the boat and Mark 4:36 (NLT) tells us they left the crowds behind. Often stepping out with Jesus will require you to leave the crowds behind, walking in faith not by sight (2 Cor. 5:7) or by feelings.

..love the LORD your God, listen to his voice, and hold fast to him. For the LORD is your life… Deut. 30:20 (NIV) Love, listen and hold fast to Him for He is your very life!

Mark 4:37 tells us a fierce storm came up. Matthew 8:24 (NLT) records it was suddenly that this occurred. Have you ever been suddenly caught off guard in one of life's fierce "storms"? What did you do and how did you perceive His faithful presence?

_____

_____

_____

Matthew 8:24 also depicts the waves crashing INTO the boat! The storm was not just outside the boat it was crashing INSIDE!! Sometimes the storm within can be more fierce than any storm without. If you feel comfortable sharing a time you felt the rage of the "storm" within please record it below and what you did and how you perceived His faithful presence in it?

_____

_____

_____

Maybe your storm rages on at this point.

Joshua 1:9 (NIV) *Have I not commanded you? Be strong and courageous. Do not be afraid; do not be discouraged, for the LORD your God will be with you wherever you go."*

"I have learned to kiss the waves that throw me up against the Rock of Ages." ~Charles H. Spurgeon

Even after the disciples had witnessed many miracles the rage of this storm had them in a panic. Often a storm has us doubting that His greatness is able to reach even that far, the fear rages that He can't or won't work. That is exactly where the enemy wants us to be, doubting God's character. In our storms we must choose to drop our anchor of trust in His faithful promises, to live in expectancy that He will work in His best way and in His best time.

We have this hope as an anchor for the soul, firm and secure. (Hebrews 6:19 NIV)

Sometimes I believe storms are allowed in order to show me He is a God who is able to calm them. I may remember His faithfulness, His greatness to me in the past and in His Word, but if I do not move forward into the application of those implications on my current circumstances I will be tossed about in the scary waves of doubt.

There are also storms allowed to show me that He is willing to work. BUT will I allow Him, or rather receive Him in a way that I learn to acknowledge His Sovereignty through it?! In every storm He is able and He will work in His best and most creative way that reveals more of His good heart to me. Will I have a heart soft enough to perceive it? Too often we are in danger of missing the revealing of more of Him and who He wants to be to us because we are only looking for the way we want Him to calm our storm or the way we expect Him to work through it when in actuality He has something so far above what we would ever ask or imagine if we would be willing to take His perspective. I pray that we are open to His better perspective in our storms.

I think God gave us the apple core to remind us of the great impact even a slight perspective shift can have. If you cut an apple vertically the core appears very, very different than if you shift it a slight quarter turn on its side and slice it through. The core now will appear in a miraculous star shape! Incredible! Miracles are everywhere... do you notice them? He will help us if we are willing.

Ezekiel 36:26 (NIV) *I will give you a new heart and put a new spirit in you; I will remove from you your heart of stone and give you a heart of flesh.*

Read Romans 1:21 and record what happens to those of us that refuse to allow Him to do heart surgery on us.

_____

_____

The NLT puts it this way, *Yes, they knew God, but they wouldn't worship him as God or even give him thanks. And they began to think up foolish ideas of what God was like. As a result, their minds became dark and confused.*

When God doesn't seem to work in a storm like we had hoped or thought He would it's easy to let our mind wander to false accusations about God. We must remember God is good all the time, He is exactly who He claims to be in His Word.

Settle your mind on His faithful promises like that in Romans 8:28 and pray for ever increasing trust. As we close today read and respond to the plea of God's heart in 1 Peter 5:7 and rest in its Truth so you can LIVE.
Please record that which has made the greatest impact on your heart from today's study of God's Word.

_____

_____

_____

_____

Day 3: Don't Give Up - Be Still

Ahoy mate! I know we ended yesterday before docking at the other side of the lake so I am extremely glad to see you have not given up but have steadfastly stayed the course. Galatians 6:9 tells us we will reap a harvest if we do not give up! Please begin in prayer that God embolden our hearts with faith and trust to follow boldly after Him no matter the cost.

For our light and momentary troubles are achieving for us an eternal glory that far outweighs them all. 2 Corinthians 4:17 (NIV)

Please, before embarking forward today, refresh your mind on yesterdays reading by briefing through Mark 4:35-41 once again. _____

Verse 41 records a question made by the disciples. Please record it below.

_____

Who is this?

Remember our study of John the Baptist and his questioning of Jesus from his viewpoint in prison. Recall how Jesus responds in Matthew 11:6?! He encourages us not to fall away from the faith because we cannot fully comprehend Him.

Mark 4:37 tells us the storms waves were threatening to fill up the boat, Luke 8:24 tells us the disciples feared drowning! Now that is quite a storm! We can allow the storm waves to drown us or we can be so filled up with the water of His word that there just isn't any room for those storm waves in our boat!

What does Jesus offer in John 4:10?

_____

Living Water
What does it do in verse John 4:14?

_____

Becomes in us a spring of water welling up to eternal LIFE!

What other hope is offered through the water of His Word in Ephesians 5:26?

_____

Cleansed, forgiven when we accept the Word. Cleansed, whether we were the cause or not.

Please look up the following verses and record the encouragement to your heart below.
Psalm 103:12 _____
Hebrews 10:22 _____
Micah 7:19 _____
Psalm 51:7 _____

2 Corinthians 5:17 _____

Isaiah 61:1-3 _____

_____

_____

_____

_____

_____

_____

Mark 4:39 tells us Jesus rebuked the wind and the waves. The wind that caused the storm and the waves, the effect of the storm. He is Lord over all, the cause and effect of any storm. Sometimes the storm is so wild I can't tell the difference between the cause and effect but He can and knows how to calm both! Praise Him for knowing what and how to pray even when I don't! Record Romans 8:26 below please.

_____

_____

After Jesus spoke there was a great calm. What can Jesus bring to our storm if we are willing to receive it? Please record Philippians 4:7 below.

_____

_____

When Jesus showed His authority over the wind and the waves we clearly see proof of His Messiahship. See Psalm 89:8-9.

Please record the questions listed in Mark 4:40 and then in 4:41.

_____

_____

Jesus asks, "Why are you afraid? Do you still have so little faith?"

The disciples ask, "Who is this man?"

If we can answer in confidence that we know "Who" stands with us in our storm, then we can find our faith, the faith that stills the fear, the worry, the anxiety, the stress…

Please record Psalm 46:10 below.

_____

_____

Be still and KNOW…

2 Timothy 1:12 (NIV) *That is why I am suffering as I am. Yet this is no cause for shame, because I know whom I have believed, and am convinced that he is able to guard what I have entrusted to him until that day.*
Please underline "I know" and "am convinced" in 2 Timothy 1:12. Let's close today in prayer that God would grant us ever increasing amounts of faith and trust in knowing Him. Knowing Him and becoming so sure of His faithfully good character as depicted in His Word that we would be immovable, unshaken by the waves of doubt no matter how long it takes to get through our storm to the other side.

I pray for you to be so absolutely convinced of His Truth, the Truth of His unfailing love for you no matter your past that you might LIVE enamored in the fullness of joy found in His free gift of salvation for your future! Salvation to an eternal paradise where no storms will ever be found!

2 Timothy 4:18 (NIV) *The Lord will rescue me from every evil attack and will bring me safely to his heavenly kingdom. To him be glory for ever and ever. Amen.*

Please recored the point of greatest impact to your heart today.

_____

_____

_____

_____

John 10:10 (NIV) *The thief comes only to steal kill and destroy; I have come that they may have life, and have it to the full.* John 8:36 (NIV) *So if the Son sets you free, you will be free indeed.*

Day 4: Hope Cycle

Hello dear one. Thank you for meeting me here today. It has been quite a journey across our stormy lake this week and today is the day we arrive safely on the other side! Please begin in prayer thanking God that He always gets us to the other side if we remain in Him.

As we wrap up the Scripture passage we began in day two of this week please refresh your mind of the whole story by choosing one of the three passages listed below to briefly sail through once more.

Matthew 8:23-27, _____ or Mark 4:35-41, _____ or Luke 8:22-25. _____

This is one boat ride I think requires a helmet!! Sometimes I think we just need to strap on our helmet and ride the cycle!! What do I mean? Well meet me on the other side of Romans 5:1-5. _____

We are supposed to do what, in trials (vs. 3)?

_____

REJOICE

Because trials help us what (vs. 3)?

_____

DEVELOP ENDURANCE

And that helps with what (vs. 4)?

_____

STRENGTH OF CHARACTER

And that strengthens what (vs. 4)?

_____

OUR CONFIDENT HOPE OF SALVATION

What kind of helmet does the armor of God have? (See Ephesians 6:17)

_____

Romans 5:5 tells us this HOPE of salvation will NOT disappoint, we can be CONFIDENT of it because we KNOW how dearly God loves us!!!

Remember the Truth you learned in day one of your study this week?! YOU are His treasure!!! He loves you dearly! As a believer you can have confident hope that your life will not end in a hopeless storm!

Please record 2 Timothy 4:18 from yesterday below.

_____

_____

When this earthly life ends your true eternal life BEGINS and He promises you will arrive safely!!! You might cannonball in but you will nail the landing, He promises! So strap on that helmet of salvation and keep your mind fixed on things above (Col. 3:2)!

Good golly my friend what do the first few words in the first verse following every single one of these accounts tell us?!? (Matt 8:28, Mark 5:1, Luke 8:26)

They arrived!!! They had crossed over to the other side just as Jesus had stated in the very beginning before they even hit the storm.

He is faithful to be who He says He will be and do what He says He will do in His Word. You dear one who believes in Jesus WILL make it through any storm arriving safely on the other side, in His Kingdom! And there, *'He will wipe every tear from their eyes. There will be no more death' or mourning or crying or pain, for the old order of things has passed away."* Revelation 21:4 (NIV) Praise the mighty, matchless, victorious name of Jesus!!

God bless you muchly for studying with me today. It has been encouraging hasn't it!

Please record the point of greatest impact to your heart today before you sign off.

Day 5: Take Me Higher Still

Welcome! Thank you for all the effort you have made to remain in this boat of study. We continue to set our sights on the goal which is to be with Him and to receive more of Him in us. I'm convinced that He will move us deeper into the true abundant life He came to give us as we trust Him to be our anchor.

Hebrews 6:19 (NIV) is a treasure to tuck into the pocket of our hearts. *We have this hope as an anchor for the soul, firm and secure. It enters the inner sanctuary behind the curtain.*

After beginning in prayer that God reveal great and unsearchable things we do not know and could never understand on our own please meet me on the other side of Matthew 8:28-34 _____, Mark 5:1-20 _____, and Luke 8:26-39. _____

These Scriptures all follow the safe arrival we studied yesterday to the other side of the Sea of Galilee of which many of those sailors highly doubted would happen in the midst of the wild storm that occurred in the middle of their journey over. Have you ever had doubts about making it through when your vantage point is from the middle of your journey… especially in the middle of a storm in the middle of your journey!?!

_____

_____

That is why we need The Rock that is higher than us! We need Someone to trust, that we know even when we can't see beyond the middle of our storm, He can and does, and promises a safe arrival in His Kingdom (2 Tim. 4:18).

We need someone bigger and higher than us to hang our hopes on. 2 Cor. 1:10 (NIV) Tells us, *He has delivered us from such a deadly peril, and he will deliver us again. On him we have set our hope that he will continue to deliver us,*

Isaiah 28:16 (NIV) tells us, *So this is what the Sovereign LORD says: "See, I lay a stone in Zion, a tested stone, a precious cornerstone for a sure foundation; the one who relies on it will never be stricken with panic.* The (NLT) ends that verse with, *…Whoever believes need never be shaken.*

We do have Someone we can hang our hopes on that is sure, regardless of our circumstance or outcome of any earthly situation. Our God does not change like shifting shadows (James 1:17) but is the tested cornerstone, sure and faithful (2 Cor. 1:18).

Just as the disciples made it through to the other side we too who hold Jesus within our boat will make it to the other side. A boat with Jesus in it will not, can not sink.

As we continue on in our study today and through next week we will face topics like demon possession, death, and disabilities bringing life into 3D for sure. We will see our God is surely the reigning power above it all!

Now back to our Scriptures for today! No sooner had they arrived safely to the other side of the lake then they were met by a demon possessed individual! Matthew is the only account that records two men, both Mark and Luke record one man. It could be that one man made a much more memorable impact. Whether there was one or two is not the point but rather that Jesus was willing to cross the gap and touch the untouchable!

This town, largely inhabited by Gentiles which would explain the herd of pigs as Jews did not raise pigs. Pigs were also considered unclean. None of this caused Jesus to hesitate in reaching out to these men.

Where does the Scripture indicate these men lived? (see Matt. 8:28)

_____

Does that seem odd to anyone else? Live in a cemetery - a cemetery is a place dead people reside. I wonder if any of us have tried living in the dead zone. Maybe it's a circumstance or situation we can't see beyond and so we have allowed the enemy to outwit us. We've bought a plot of hopelessness to live in a shell of death though we have life still to live; the gift of a breath in our lungs and a beat in our heart proves it!

These men came out to meet Jesus as He arrived. Jesus has arrived for us too. Will we choose to come out from among the dead to live the life He still has for us beyond what we deemed hopeless? Dear one, may we grasp that He has a hope that will not disappoint (Romans 5:5)!

According to Matthew 8:29 these demons knew Jesus was/is the Son of the Most High God and were also well aware their time was/is limited! What happens when you know time is running out, maybe on a work project or something?

_____

When a deadline approaches the level of intensity to complete the work amps up right! The enemy knows his time is limited and the closer we get to the end he is going to amp up his tactics to outwit and distract us from our purpose and ultimate destination in God's Kingdom!

Please read Jude 1:6 _____ and Revelation 20:10. _____
Now read Romans 13:11-14 and record the encouragement in that wake up call.

_____

_____

In Mark 5:9-13 Who is clearly depicted having the upper hand?

_____

A legion of demons was still no match for the Son of the Most High God Who holds ultimate power and authority over them.

In Mark 5:17 what was the town's response to how Jesus cured these men?

_____

Could we too be in the same boat if we are not careful? Becoming too concerned with our worldly state of being that we miss the mission He created our lives for?

Will we allow Him to finish the work He started in our lives regardless of the cost to us here on earth knowing that we in reality are on mission to the Kingdom where there is no heartache, crying or pain (Rev. 21:4)?!

Remember the statement Jesus made to John the Baptist in Matthew 11:6? Please record it once again on the line below.

_____

God help us to trust Your eyes, Your ears and Your heart that see, hear and understand far beyond ourselves. We want to live the adventure, brave the storm knowing You are always with us and in You our adventure only ends in Paradise on the other side! Oh Heavenly Father take us higher still, farther still, that you might increase the population of Heaven through our surrendered lives to Yours.

Please close today resting in the Truth of Isaiah 43:2. _____

Matthew 16:25 (NIV) *For whoever wants to save their life will lose it, but whoever loses their life for me will find it.*

Please record the point that made the greatest impact on your heart through your study of His Word today.

_____

_____

_____

_____

Day 6 & 7: At His Feet - A Time to Reflect

Over the next two days take time to reflect over your week of study. Maybe you need some time to catch up on the study material and this might be the perfect break to do just that with the Lord!

I encourage you to glance back at the final point at the end of each day that you recorded having had the greatest impact on your heart. As you spend time with God in prayer, reflect and record on the lines below how God is tying it all together and applying it to your life.

Ask that God make it clear who He would have you invite into a natural opportunity to share Him, to apply what you are learning. Trust Him to continue to take the lead. May we have a heart ever ready with eyes and ears out to the opportunities God wants to invite us into for His glory and praise.

Do not merely listen to the word, and so deceive yourselves. Do what it says. Anyone who listens to the word but does not do what it says is like someone who looks at his face in a mirror and, after looking at himself, goes away and immediately forgets what he looks like. But whoever looks intently into the perfect law that gives freedom, and continues in it - not forgetting what they have heard, but doing it - they will be blessed in what they do.
James 1:22-25 (NIV)

_____

_____

_____

Philippians 4:13 (NIV) *I can do all things through him who gives me strength.*
John 14:26 (NIV) *But the Advocate, the Holy Spirit, whom the Father will send in my name, will teach you all things and will remind you of everything I have said to you.*

WEEK 3

from the end of the earth I call to you when my heart is faint. Lead me to the rock that is higher than I, Psalm 61:2 (ESV)

Day 1: Life In 3D

Welcome to week three! Thank you for diligently continuing in His Word with me. *...the Scriptures give us hope and encouragement as we wait patiently for God's promises to be fulfilled.* Romans 15:4 (NLT) I do pray you feel the hope and encouragement from His Word refresh your soul. Let's bow before God Almighty, our Rock, and ask that He continue to faithfully lead us through, strengthening us to follow in obedience as we LIVE for His glory.

Before we go any further I think tucking 2 Timothy 1:7 from the NKJV into our hearts pocket would be most appropriate for our journey. *For God has not given us a spirit of fear, but of power and of love and of a sound mind.*

Please take a moment to recall our Scripture reading from day 5 last week. Please briefly read ONE of the following to refresh your memory from where we left off last week. Matthew 8:28-34 _____, or Mark 5:1-20 _____, or Luke 8:26-39. _____

These people wanted Jesus to leave their region. I'm reminded of another people that complained against the goodness of God. Please read Numbers 21:4-9. _____

What do the people do that causes snakes to enter their community and wreak havoc?

_____

The people sinned against God. They complained about Him and the way He was providing for them! So God pulls back handing them over to themselves and snakes were allowed in and were biting everyone literally to death!
We currently live in a broken world and "snakes will bite". Why? Because humans invited sin into the world way back in Genesis 3. No matter who you are you will experience trouble in this world (John 16:33). It's what we do with the bite that matters.

Check out Acts 28:1-6 _____.
First off let's not miss what drove out that snake! Verse 3 tells me that viper was driven out by the heat!! Jeremiah 23:29 relays to me God's declaration of His Word to be like fire!!! I don't know about you but that ignites a passion to stoke up in my heart the heat of His Truth-FULL Word that will dispel any and all lies from my mind making it a sound one as 2 Timothy 1:7 indicates is mine in Jesus!

In Acts we read that Paul shook off the snake that bit him into the fire. This opened an opportunity to reach those that had suffered similarly. When we suffer along the way to the Kingdom we can see it as an opportunity to show compassion to others suffering similarly; to show God-confidence that He will be faithful in His presence and sufficient grace throughout our trial.

In Numbers how were the people healed (21:8-9)?

_____

They looked to the bronze snake. This instance and meaning came to light many years later in John 3:14-15. Oftentimes it will not be till much later that we see the benefit or good come from our suffering. Sometimes it will not be till heaven that we will fully understand all the good, God brought about through our trials of suffering. However I do know as we submit to His way we will ever be conforming to the image of His Son and that is the very best thing we could ever be.

Though the true fulfillment of the cure for sin came not in Numbers but in John, so too, the fulfillment of all God's promises will come to pass. They are all fulfilled in Jesus Christ. So when we are bitten by the "snakes" of life and we are left wondering, we too can shake them off into the fiery truth of His promises. Though we wonder, we need not waiver. Don't allow Satan a chance to outwit us and keep us in a shell of death when we were meant for life.

I truly love the picture the NLT paints of this formerly demon possessed man in Luke 8:35, ...*He was sitting at Jesus' feet, fully clothed and perfectly sane,...*

Jesus had restored this man by His word through His heart of compassion for all who are lost. This man, who was considered untouchable, unclean, was made new in Jesus. He had gotten back His mind, His sound mind in an instant by the Word of Jesus. Not only that but what was he given in Luke 8:38-39?

_____

A mission! God had not only healed him, set him free, restored his mind but saw GREAT purpose for his life beyond his captivity in the death zone!!!

No matter where you have been or what you have been through, God still sees your life worthy of a mission on His field. *What, then, shall we say in response to these things? If God is for us, who can be against us? Romans 8:31 (NIV)*

Dear one, please record what impacted your heart most from todays study of God's Word.

_____

_____

_____

_____

Day 2: Be Amazed

Welcome back my friend. We are going to jump right in where we left off in the gospel books but first let us bow in prayer that our God of Light lead and illuminate our way.

For with you is the fountain of life; in your light we see light. Psalm 36:9 (NIV)

Please proceed to our next bundle of Scripture readings. Matthew 9:18-26 _____, Mark 5:21-43 _____, Luke 8:40-56. _____

Let's look and be amazed that not only is our God stronger than the devil and his legions but He is also the overcomer of death and disgrace! Yesterday was titled "Life in 3D" and when life comes out at us in seemingly 3D ways full of the devil, death, disgrace and things of the like… may we remember we have a God larger than life and has overcome this world across all dimensions! (See Colossians 2:15)

In these Scriptures we see two healings take place. What are they?

_____

_____

As a parent I don't believe there could be a bigger trial than the life and death issue of your child. This is what Jairus was facing and at any cost would do anything to save his daughter. He displays faith as he falls at the feet of Jesus (Mark 5:22). As a synagogue leader he was likely to know some Pharisees and I would imagine would not have been exempt from the rising pressure to avoid supporting Jesus let alone be found bowing before him!

Later in Mark 5:36 Jesus sees the need to encourage Jairus' faith. What does He say?

_____

This encouragement comes on the heels of what event (Mark 5:35)?

_____

Jairus is told his daughter is dead. When humanly speaking it appears hope is gone Jesus reaches out as our LIVING HOPE (1 Peter 1:3) and says, keep the faith.

What is the crowd doing during this critical time of wavering faith? Are they helping or hurting?

_____

The crowd of people laughed at Jesus' word of hope. So what did Jesus do with them (Mark 5:40)?

_____

Jesus asked them to leave. Sometimes we have to root out what is weakening our faith so we do not become distracted or discouraged from our purpose in Christ.

Jesus held this 12 year old girl's hand and told her to get up even though she was presumed dead by all humanity. What happened (Mark 5:42)?

_____

Like the demon possessed man that fell at Jesus' feet perfectly sane after Jesus' interaction with Him this girl's transformation was immediate!! From death to life just like that! From insane to sane just like that! He is the God of the impossible because He is I-AM-possible!

What in your life can you believe Him to be your I-AM-possible?

_____

_____

God is at work working all things out for the very, very best way which so happens to be WAY beyond us!

Trust the One who holds the good plans. (See Jeremiah 29:11)

Please record what impacted your heart the most from your time in His Word today.

_____

_____

_____

_____

Day 3: His Touch

Hello friend, I'm so glad you are back! Today we are going to wade through our Scriptures from yesterday and take a different focus angle. First let us begin in prayer that our God clear all distractions from our heart and mind in order to be open to receiving His angle for our hearts from todays study.

We can tuck this one into our hearts pocket: Daniel 2:22 (NIV) *He reveals deep and hidden things; he knows what lies in darkness, and light dwells with him.*

Before preceding please briefly review your Scriptures from yesterday just to refresh our minds in the Living Word. Matthew 9:18-26 _____, Mark 5:21-43 _____, Luke 8:40-56. _____

Between Jairus falling at the feet of Jesus, begging Him to come heal his daughter and the daughter's miraculous healing, who does Jesus encounter?

A woman suffering for 12 years, just as long as the little girl had been alive. If it seems you have been suffering a lifetime, hope lives even in that time of life. Luke 8:44 (NLT) states, *Coming up behind Jesus, she touched the fringe of his robe. Immediately, the bleeding stopped.*

In verse 48 the woman is commended for her faith by Jesus. I wonder if she went back to what she knew in Malachi 4:2 and acted in faith based on what His Word said?

But for you who fear my name, the sun of righteousness shall rise with healing in its wings. You shall go out leaping like calves from the stall. Malachi 4:2 (ESV)

Please circle the word "wings" in the above verse. That word "wings" in Hebrew is [2]kanaph and can refer to an edge of a garment.

If this woman who had tried EVERYTHING else under the sun and had no success remembered Malachi 4:2 I believe she took a flying leap of faith for that fringe having found one last glimmer of hope!

Luke 8:47 (NLT) states, ...*The whole crowd heard her explain why she had touched him and that she had been immediately healed.* I wonder if her explanation included Malachi 4:2 and her leap of faith revealing the faithfulness of His Word! To which Jesus says, go in peace, your faith has made you well.

---

[2] Malachi 4 (KJV) - But unto you that fear. Retrieved from https://www.blueletterbible.org/kjv/mal/4/2/p0/ss1/t_conc_929002

Even when we do not receive the answer to prayer that we want, it's our faith and trust in the One who holds and gives us His best answer always (even when we don't understand it) that keeps us "perfectly sane", that makes us immediately well in our soul.

Please meet me on the other side of Matthew 9:27-34. _____

In this passage what two disabilities are healed?

_____

When the deaf hear and the mute speak signs of the Kingdom are revealed. (See Matthew 11:3-5)

His transformation of a life can be instant and absolute. Praise Him!

What is the question Jesus asks in Matthew 9:28?

_____

Do you believe I can make you see?

If Jesus asked you that question what would you say? Do you believe I can make you see hope after failure, despair, heartache? Do you believe I can make you see life after tragedy? Do you believe I can make you see you are worth more than you know because I love you more than you know?

I pray that from his glorious, unlimited resources he will empower you with inner strength through his Spirit. Then Christ will make his home in your hearts as you trust in him. Your roots will grow down into God's love and keep you strong. And may you have the power to understand, as all God's people should, how wide, how long, how high, and how deep his love is. May you experience the love of Christ, though it is too great to understand fully. Then you will be made complete with all the fullness of life and power that comes from God.
Ephesians 3:16-19 (NLT)

When life comes at you in 3D when you specifically requested the ticket for the flat screen experience remember our God has capital D, Defeated the devil, death and disease so we can face 3D and, never be shaken (Isaiah 28:16)!

Please record what impacted your heart the most before signing off today dear one and thank you muchly for joining me!

_____

_____

_____

_____

Day 4: Reason to Rejoice

We had a pet butterfly for a while once. My children picked up a caterpillar in a jar one day and it just so happened that, that very night the caterpillar spun its cocoon within that jar! Now I didn't know this before then but a caterpillar that makes its cocoon late in the season (and it was late in the season) can actually hibernate in the cocoon!! So we ended up caring for that little guy's cocoon for some time… until one day months later he emerged!! We named him Hupo, short for hupomone which is Greek for patient endurance. His name's sake verse was Romans 12:12 a good one to tuck in our hearts pocket today actually!

Romans 12:12 (NIV) *Be joyful in hope, patient in affliction, faithful in prayer.*

Let's begin today faithful in prayer asking that God lead our hearts and make them willing to follow Him.

Please meet me on the other side of Matthew 13:53-58 _____ and Mark 6:1-6.

_____

What was the peoples first emotional response to Jesus' teaching (Mark 6:2)?

_____

What was their second response almost immediately (Mark 6:3)?

_____

Amazed and in the next breath offended!!

The only way to lead is to step out from the crowd. The very moment that happens you become a target! However if God has called you out, then there is nothing that can prevail against His purpose through you.

What was God's response to the prophet Jeremiah in Jeremiah chapter 12:5-6 when he had experienced conflict from men?

_____

Rise up! If this running with men makes you tired how will you take on the horses because one thing leadership is not going to get is easier! But praise God His measure of strength matches if not exceeds our weakness!

Please record 2 Corinthians 9:8 below.

_____

_____

Please circle all the words "all" and "every" in that verse.

Please read what happens to the apostle Paul in Acts 22:1-23._____

Compare Acts 22:21 with Luke 2:28-32.
Simeon had a heart to perceive Truth far sooner than most. At Jesus' dedication Simeon knew Jesus was a gift to all nations even to the Gentiles. A Truth most missed yet was spoken from the beginning. See Genesis 12:1-3.

____

In the promise God gave Abraham He indicates His promise of eternal blessing is for ALL nations, ALL people! Simeon could die in peace as he had experienced the fulfillment of God's promise to him. God would continue to work out the fulfillment of reaching ALL people even the Gentiles through Paul's life. Was it easy, no. Did Paul fear his life was at stake, I'm sure many times yes. Did God prove faithful in providing and preserving to accomplish His purpose and promise, yes... every time all throughout history. What does Paul say in your own words in Philippians 1:18-26?

_____

_____

_____

God Almighty is worth it.

History is clearly HIS-story and nothing will thwart His plot line which is for EVERY tribe tongue and nation to be in heaven with Him. How has He asked you to participate in His mission for reaching EVERYone for Him? What might be holding you back that you can lay at His feet, allowing His shoulders to lift what is too heavy or too difficult and complicated?

_____

_____

Revelation 7:9 (NIV) *After this I looked, and there before me was a great multitude that no one could count, from every nation, tribe, people and language, standing before the throne and before the Lamb. They were wearing white robes and were holding palm branches in their hands.*

Now read Hebrews 4:15-16 and record how this emboldens your faith and trust in Him in regards to any current challenges you may be facing.

_____

_____

_____

But he said to me, "My grace is sufficient for you, for my power is made perfect in weakness." Therefore I will boast all the more gladly of my weaknesses, so that the power of Christ may rest upon me. 2 Corinthians 12:9 (ESV)

Our weakness is not too strong for His strength! In closing today please read Matthew 5:11-12 and record below the reason we can rejoice in suffering.

_____

Thank you for your diligence today in His Word. Please record what had the greatest impact on your heart.

_____

_____

_____

_____

Day 5: Ask - Send - Go

Welcome and well done my friend! You have just about concluded your third week of an in-depth study of God's Word! I pray we both perceive His faithfulness as we submit to His application of it in our lives. Please begin today's study in prayer before preceding.

...Those who honor me I will honor... 1 Samuel 2:30 (NIV)

Please read Matthew 9:35-38. _____

How does verse 36 describe the crowds?

_____

Like a sheep without a shepherd.

Leadership is not easy but it is needed. 2 Corinthians 10:13 reveals we all have a sphere of influence, a circle within which God has called us to lead for Him in a way He Himself has defined for us. Maybe it's keeping house, raising children, volunteering in the nursery or to teach Sunday School. Maybe it's in an office or on a sport team. Every job handed to you by the King of kings is important and valuable to His Kingdom. It can be easy to become riddled in the middle. Just because we may not be the lead sled dog, so to speak, in our arenas let us not succumb to the temptation to think that our influence is any less impactful. Sometimes the greatest things are done in the smallest ways behind the scenes… like a baby born in a manger. What He purposes He will provide for and nothing can mess with the outcome of His master plan.

Please record both Colossians 3:23-24 and 1 Corinthians 15:58 below.

_____

_____

_____

_____

In Matthew 9:37 what does Jesus say is great or plentiful?

_____

The harvest or the multitudes of people that need to hear His Good News! Too often we allow our focus to be taken up by the world's "breaking news" and that usually does just that… breaks us.

So what are we to do about it (verse 38)?

_____

All ministry is under God's call so ask God to call more workers, embolden more leaders willing to do the hard thing the right way as working for God Almighty and not for human masters!

For the eyes of the LORD range throughout the earth to strengthen those whose hearts are fully committed to him…. 2 Chronicles 16:9 (NIV)

Please read our next segment of Scripture. Matthew 10:1-15 _____, Mark 6:6-13 _____, and Luke 9:1-6. _____

The 12 men listed in Matthew were not accidentally called just as you are not accidentally called. The number 12 resembles the 12 tribes of Israel, these are God's new leaders to bring the Good News to the world.

What are you doing right now that you feel is fulfilling God's calling on your life?

_____

_____

Sometimes I think I can overcomplicate this concept of trying to decipher God's call. Could it be as simple as walking into a room, noticing a need, a need that I could meet well and then just stepping forward in God-confidence to meet it?
What are these men warned of in Matthew 10:14?

_____

Not everywhere you go will accept you or your message. The same is true for us. Does that mean we are going the wrong direction, that we misunderstood God's call on our life? No! It does mean we need to be faithful in prayer, ready to receive encouragement, equipping, redirection or warning at any time.

Dear one you have been called, you are an answer to someone's prayer, keep following Him out into the "harvest field"!

Please record the point of greatest impact to your heart today.

_____

_____

_____

_____

Day 6 & 7: At His Feet - A Time to Reflect

Over the next two days take time to reflect over your week of study. Maybe you need some time to catch up on the study material and this might be the perfect break to do just that with the Lord!

I encourage you to glance back at the final point at the end of each day that you recorded having had the greatest impact on your heart. As you spend time with God in prayer, reflect and record on the lines below how God is tying it all together and applying it to your life.

Ask that God make it clear who He would have you invite into a natural opportunity to share Him, to apply what you are learning. Trust Him to continue to take the lead. May we have a heart ever ready with eyes and ears out to the opportunities God wants to invite us into for His glory and praise.

Do not merely listen to the word, and so deceive yourselves. Do what it says. Anyone who listens to the word but does not do what it says is like someone who looks at his face in a mirror and, after looking at himself, goes away and immediately forgets what he looks like. But whoever looks intently into the perfect law that gives freedom, and continues in it - not forgetting what they have heard, but doing it - they will be blessed in what they do.
James 1:22-25 (NIV)

_____

_____

_____

_____

_____

Philippians 4:13 (NIV) *I can do all things through him who gives me strength.*

John 14:26 (NIV) *But the Advocate, the Holy Spirit, whom the Father will send in my name, will teach you all things and will remind you of everything I have said to you.*

WEEK 4

When you pass through the waters, I will be with you; and when you pass through the rivers, they will not sweep over you. When you walk through the fire, you will not be burned; the flames will not set you ablaze. Isaiah 43:2 (NIV)

Day 1: Warning

Hello dear friend, welcome back. I think it's fair to say, there is a lot of unfairness in the world today, right! But grace is not fair and aren't we glad it's not because none of us could receive it if it was. Grace is not fair, it is undeserved favor. In the grand scheme of life we have all been offered the greatest gift of grace of all time through the cross. Somehow though along the way we can get tripped up because we think we deserve more. If we get nothing else than the Son of God sacrificing Himself on the cross in our place to give us a free spot in paradise for eternity... I think it's fair to say we sure lucked out!

However not to downplay the serious and tragic happenings in life this side of heaven that just truly are not right. Sin entered our world because we humans brought it in (Gen. 3), our good God activated (by His saving grace) our rescue. We live in a broken world but we have paradise on it's way!

And he who was seated on the throne said, "Behold, I am making all things new." Also he said, "Write this down, for these words are trustworthy and true." Revelation 21:5 (ESV) Let us tuck this one in our hearts pocket today because even when He doesn't make our current situation "new" or our day "new and improved" like we might have hoped, we still have an opportunity to allow Him to make our heart new. New within the old and crummy situation that in His ultimate wisdom and way He has chosen to allow to remain unchanged.

Therefore, change your hearts and stop being stubborn. "For the LORD your God is the God of gods and Lord of lords. He is the great God, the mighty and awesome God, who shows no partiality and cannot be bribed. Deuteronomy 10:16-17 (NLT)

Let's bow and pray our great, mighty and awesome God lead us and help us to obediently follow Him through His Word today. Let's ask that He still our distractions bringing us into His quietness allowing His Truth to wash over our hearts and minds in a way that we truly sense His nearness and begin to take hold of the true power of His resurrection within us. To Him be the glory.

Please meet me on the other side of Matthew 10:16-42. _____

In verses 16-25 please list all the warnings you hear below.

_____

_____

_____

_____

My list of warnings includes: wolves, floggings, trials, arrests, betrayal, rebellion, death, hate, persecution, called worse names than even the prince of demons! BUT what encouragement do you hear God give in these same verses?

_____

_____

_____

_____

My list includes: Don't worry - God will give to us as needed, even the right words at the right time - open opportunities to proclaim the Gospel - enduring to the end we will be saved thus in spite it all we have a happy ending! Like Simeon who remained steadfast in the promise of God (Luke 2:25-32)! No matter how high the waves of doubt may have grown, he was able to end in peace because those whose minds are steadfast in trust, will keep in PERFECT peace (Isaiah 26:3).

In Matthew 10:26-31 what are we told not to fear and why?

_____

_____

_____

_____

My list includes: Not to fear those who threaten you because one day all will be revealed - Don't be afraid of those that can kill the body because they can't touch your soul - Don't be afraid because you are just so incredibly valuable to the Father -

List any other warnings you hear in verses 32-42.

_____

_____

_____

_____

My list includes: count the cost, it clearly won't be a cake walk but it will be well worth every step - Don't be diluted by false expectations and an attitude of entitlement, Jesus requires a choice and that will bring a sword between those who choose life and those who by way of rejecting Him have chosen death - to follow Him requires caring a cross, dying to self and living the life He died to give you, abundant life that is only found free from self-centeredness.

How does this passage end?

_____

_____

I feel like Zechariah 2:8-9 is a good summary for the end of this passage in Matthew.

(NLT) *After a period of glory, the LORD of Heaven's Armies sent me against the nations who plundered you. For he said, "Anyone who harms you harms my most precious possession. I will raise my fist to crush them, and their own slaves will plunder them." Then you will know the LORD of Heaven's Armies has sent me.*

God's warning is clear against the enemy that would come against us but it is also clear to us. The journey will not be easy but honestly this life is not easy for anyone this side of heaven, but it may even seem harder in some ways for those that choose to follow Jesus. HOWEVER it's also clear we don't fight for the victory, in Jesus that is already ours! He fought for us and won that battle at the cross!

When you were dead in your sins and in the uncircumcision of your flesh, God made you alive with Christ. He forgave us all our sins, having canceled the charge of our legal indebtedness, which stood against us and condemned us; he has taken it away, nailing it to the cross. And having disarmed the powers and authorities, he made a public spectacle of them, triumphing over them by the cross. Colossians 2:13-15 (NIV)

Praise the One who reigns even still, even when, and even if...

This world is a battlefield warring over the free choice of human souls. What will the final population count be of our eternal destination?

May we consider the cost and yet still choose to be counted among the weak made strong in Him to carry our cross for the One who carried ours all the way to hell so we would never have to.

Thank you dear one for today. Please record the piece that made the most impact to your heart before signing off.

_____

_____

_____

_____

Day 2: It's Just Not Fair

Welcome back my friend. We opened this week speaking of unfairness and in a moment we will revisit that thought however please bow with me before we jump in praising God that the gift of grace is free and not fair. If grace was a gift given in fairness not one of us would be able to receive it.

Thanks be to God for his indescribable gift! 2 Corinthians 9:15 (NIV)

Please read this story that from every vantage point, makes us all want to cry, "UNFAIR!". Matthew 14:3-13 _____ and Mark 6:17-29. _____

Matthew 14:10 (NLT) *So John was beheaded in the prison,* AAAAHH!!!!!! NOOO! NOT FAIR!!! Anyone else feel twisted up inside when they read that verse?!

Jesus Himself did too I think as we read Matthew 14:13 (NLT) *As soon as Jesus heard the news, he left in a boat to a remote area to be alone....*

We too need to deal with our grief without allowing our grief to deal with us. Praise that in our weakest He is strongest (2 Cor. 12:9) because grief is something bearable only on the shoulders of One who is stronger. Jesus withdrew but then by verse 14 He is stepping out of the boat, with eyes on others and moved with compassion, began to heal them! He begins to minister to others out of His broken heart.

Blessed be the God and Father of our Lord Jesus Christ, the Father of mercies and God of all comfort, who comforts us in all our affliction, so that we may be able to comfort those who are in any affliction, with the comfort with which we ourselves are comforted by God. 2 Corinthians 1:3-4 (ESV)

What does Mark 6:17-19 tell us about why everyone was out to get John?

_____

Just like the religious leaders were offended or felt threatened by the ministry of Jesus and sought to take Him down and have Him killed rather than repent and deal with their sin, such is it with these political leaders attacking John! Not fair! The good guys are supposed to win!

Oh dear one we do win! Please read Psalm 73 paying close attention to verse 17. This writer also questioned why it seemed the evil was getting ahead but it was when he went "where" according to verse 17, that he realized the ultimate fate of evil?

_____

Things become clear as we too come and abide in Jesus, in His Word and in prayer.

According to verses 21-22 what else is revealed to the Psalmist in chapter 73?

_____

When we come near to Him not only can He make things clear without but also reveal and make clear things within. Only the One who knit us together in our mothers womb is familiar with our subconscious parts. Only He knows how to reveal and heal ALL the parts.

Please read 1 Corinthians 15:54-57 and record what has been defeated and how for those that believe Jesus is Who His Word says He is?

_____

What is the fate of those who choose not to believe according to Matthew 13:41-42 (go ahead and read through verse 43)?

_____

This world is a battle zone and every human must choose what side they fight from...victory or defeat. The victory has already been won at the cross but the fight for the population total of heaven and hell is still on. Christians must choose their battle ground.

In Mark 6:26 what state of emotion was Herod in when he made the decision to have John killed?

_____

He caved under pressure from his friends (some friends right). Take a moment to fast forward to Mark 15:15 and record who and at what scene does someone else cave to pressure?

_____

Before Herod caved under pressure what did he offer the daughter that danced for him at his birthday party (Mark 6:22-23)?

_____

Funny thing is he didn't even have half the kingdom to give her! He himself was under Roman authority. It was his way of saying she could pretty much have anything she wanted. Have you ever underestimated the power of words?

_____

James 3:8 (NIV) *but no human being can tame the tongue. It is a restless evil, full of deadly poison.* Yikes! That is a warning we all should heed.

What good advice does Proverbs 15:1 give us?

_____

For fools speak foolishness and make evil plans… Isaiah 32:6 (NLT)

Please jump back up to Matthew 14:1-2 _____ and Mark 6:14-16. _____

In the story recorded by Mark there is much speculation as to who Jesus is. No matter who people THINK Jesus is, never for one moment changes Who He remains to be, God Almighty the Savior of the World.

Before we close today please read Luke 9:7-9. _____

Verse 9 in the NLT states, "I beheaded John," Herod said, "so who is this man about whom I hear such stories?" And he kept trying to see him.

Because John had passed away who was it really that Herod was so curious about and "kept trying to see"?!?

_____

JESUS!

In all that we would feel the urge to cry out "UNFAIR!" in, by the grace of God Almighty I pray He please help us to trust Him who IS good and is working a plan out that will be more beautiful than we could comprehend. Trust that one day all that what we can't make sense of now will make perfect sense (1 Cor. 13:12). In the meantime surrendering our grief to His stronger shoulders, allowing Him to restart our heart if need be with compassion for others needs around us, to look up, to step out of the boat once again and keep living because there are others that are still "trying to see" Jesus. Someone needs the Light you have inside.

The light shines in the darkness, and the darkness has not overcome it. John 1:5 (NIV)

Remember the words spoken to John by Jesus when John had questions surrounding his current circumstances from prison… *Blessed is anyone who does not stumble on account of me."* Matthew 11:6 (NIV)

Yet the LORD longs to be gracious to you; therefore he will rise up to show you compassion. For the LORD is a God of justice. Blessed are all who wait for him! Isaiah 30:18 (NIV)

He has given us His Light - ultimately that's unfair but praise God Almighty for somethings like grace, that are… UNFAIR!
Please record what made the greatest impact on your heart today.

_____

_____

_____

_____

Day 3: How Much Do You Have?

Hello my friend, are you still wrestling out the truths of yesterday's study too? Let's begin today praying to surrender to His leading. *Teach me your way, LORD, that I may rely on your faithfulness; give me an undivided heart, that I may fear your name.* Psalm 86:11 (NIV)

Let's jump right into our passages today as we have all four gospels giving an account on the event we will study first. Matthew 14:13-21 _____, Mark 6:30-44 _____, Luke 9:10-17 _____ and John 6:1-15. _____

The New Testament continues (as we know) to faithfully support the fact that Jesus is the fulfillment of all the Old Testament. See Acts 3:17-18.

This feeding the 5,000 event foreshadows the feast at salvation for all nations! Take a moment to savor the good news of Isaiah 25:6-9!

In John 6:2 we see the people are following Jesus why?

_____

They had seen what He could do. So on top of the grief of losing a good friend, John the Baptist, He has the added weight of feeling like the friends that are left are really only seeking Him for what He could do for them and not for just who He was.

When we go to Him is it usually to see what He can or will do for us or is it to just abide in a relationship with our Heavenly Father, to give Him our love and appreciate His?

_____

We can pray that He stir up in our hearts a craving in ever increasing amounts to just be with Him for Him and not because of what we can get from Him.

In spite of all the valid reasons Jesus could have given to step back from His ministry, from serving us, He instead steps forward.

Of course there are times for resting, the Sabbath was created because God knew we would need time to retreat into Him alone. There are also times when we need to look up, step out and allow God to revive our hearts with compassion for others to a point that we continue serving in the strength and energy He promises to provide for His purpose. What does Jesus teach about in Luke 9:11?

He WELCOMES them (and I'm sure it wasn't with a heavy sigh and a roll of the eyes) Jesus welcomes the crowds and begins teaching them about the Kingdom.

And if the Spirit of him who raised Jesus from the dead is living in you, he who raised Christ from the dead will also give life to your mortal bodies because of his Spirit who lives in you. Romans 8:11 (NIV)

How different would our lives look if we remembered that His resurrection power is within us!!!

Please record Luke 17:21 below.

In the beginning of Mark's rendition the apostles have just returned to Jesus from their ministry tour, telling Him all they had done and taught… however when they are faced with this new predicament of finding food for people they seem to have forgotten so quickly the power that was with them on their tour is the same able power with them now!

Sometimes when we begin to feel the waves of doubt and fear begin to roll inside of us the best anchor for our rocking ship is to remember how God has been faithful in the past AND then recognize and receive the implications of that over our current situations.

We can always hang our hope on God who is faithful. *Therefore, since we have such a hope, we are very bold.* 2 Corinthians 3:12 (NIV)

In 2 Corinthians 1:9-10 (NIV) you can hear Paul's bold God-confidence! *Indeed, we felt we had received the sentence of death. But this happened that we might not rely on ourselves but on God, who raises the dead. He has delivered us from such a deadly peril, and he will deliver us again. On him we have set our hope that he will continue to deliver us,*

Oh to live life with such bold courageous confidence in the Almighty God in us - what an adventure life becomes!!!

In Mark 6:37 Jesus tells the disciples to do what?

_____

Feed the masses. They respond, "With what?"!!! Can you just picture that moment everyone looking at one another like should we laugh or is He serious?!.. Oh good golly He IS serious!! They begin to protest that it's just impossible (forgetting so quickly all the amazingly impossible work He just did through these unqualified individuals on their ministry tour just as we so often do). Mark 6:38 (NLT) records Jesus' response this way, *"How much bread do you have?" he asked. "Go and find out."...*

Jesus tells us He is the Bread of Life (John 6:35). How much Bread do you have? Ephesians 3:19 tells us we can be filled with all the fullness of God. How filled up are you with Him? Sometimes we don't really know until we "go and find out", will we step out in faith and trust Him to be enough in us? Are we willing to empty ourselves of us enough to make room for Him; more of Him?

Is there an area in your life where you feel like the same question is being asked of you? How much Bread do you have? You can have as much as you want but how much do you have?

_____

_____

Go and find out dear one, go and find out... Find He is faithful and upon Him you can always hang your hope.

Thank you for traveling through His Word with me today, I'm already looking forward to seeing you back here tomorrow! Go ahead and record that piece of information God impacted your heart with the most today before signing off. Thanks again!

_____

_____

_____

_____

Day 4: Source of Sustenance

Hi! I'm so grateful you made it back here today. I know the distractions of this world can be 3D and in your face so I commend you for lifting your eyes and tuning your ears into the voice of Truth calling your name. *Whether you turn to the right or to the left, your ears will hear a voice behind you, saying, "This is the way; walk in it."* Isaiah 30:21 (NIV)

Please first bow in prayer before our God that He would take the lead in our hearts as He enables us to follow.

Picking up right where we left off yesterday you may want to briefly run over the Scriptures we are focusing on just to refresh that brain.

Matthew 14:13-21 _____, Mark 6:30-44 _____, Luke 9:10-17 _____ and John 6:1-15. _____

We left off yesterday at the moment Jesus was asking His men just how much they had to give the crowd. (Mark 6:37) Our greatest gift to anyone will be His Spirit within us.

The disciples go and find out what kind of access they had to any food and John records Andrew with the courage to bring a boy's small lunch to Jesus as ridiculous as it may seem to everyone, ...*what good is that with this huge crowd?"* John 6:9 NLT

How often are we held back from sharing, giving, serving, helping because we fear that what we have to offer is not enough or good enough? As we continue we will see they didn't give to the crowd anything they first had not turned over to God's hand. Anything we have, little as it may seem, when first filtered through His hand, will ALWAYS be enough. What might you have to trust into His hands?

_____

_____

Jesus welcomes the disciples meager offering and asks everyone to sit down; why? Because He is always doing things in a fitting and orderly way (1 Cor. 14:40).

...*Then, breaking the loaves into pieces, he kept giving the bread and fish to the disciples so they could distribute it to the people.* Luke 9:16 (NLT) Please circle the phrase "he kept giving" and "so they could distribute".

Please record how 2 Corinthians 9:11 affirms this thought of always having enough to continue to give out.

_____

_____

Please circle the second word in Luke 9:16 as recorded above and write it here. _____ Have you ever experienced a time of "breaking" that resulted in widening your sphere of influence and ended up providing multiple opportunities to share Jesus in you with others that you never would have had otherwise?

_____

_____

_____

Don't let the enemy outwit you and talk you into letting a "breaking" make you feel disqualified but rather seek God's heart on how this qualifies you for new opportunities to shine His healing, redeeming, miraculous and loving Light!

Let's not let the lack of resources within ourselves hinder us from stepping out by faith into the Source, trusting Him to be and provide all we'll ever need. He is all sufficient. That day Jesus fed the people's spiritual need without overlooking their physical needs. That is effective ministry. What does James 2:14-17 tell us about properly ministering to others' needs?

_____

_____

Do to others as you would have them do to you. Luke 6:31 (NLT)

If everyone got fed that day it would have been miracle enough, however how does God go above and beyond?

_____

There are LEFTOVERS! 12 baskets leftover. The 12 disciples gave all they had and ended up with more than they could imagine! *Now to him who is able to do immeasurably more than all we ask or imagine, according to his power that is at work within us, to him be glory in the church and in Christ Jesus throughout all generations, for ever and ever! Amen.* Ephesians 3:20-21 (NIV)

God is able to put His Eph. 3:20 stamp on any situation, circumstance and/or life. How well do we leave God room, through our faith and trust, to use it in/on our lives? On others' lives?

Praying to live with expectancy rather than in my expectation. We don't want to miss our God looking for how we expect Him to show up. Keep your desires and delights centered on Him who remains faithfully the Source of all sustenance.

Give, and it will be given to you. A good measure, pressed down, shaken together and running over, will be poured into your lap. For with the same measure you use, it will be measured to you." Luke 6:38 (NIV)

Please record how your heart was impacted the most from your time studying His Word today.

_____

_____

_____

_____

Day 5: Wave Walker

Hello friend! I hope you brought your galoshes for todays set of Scripture readings! Please begin in prayer and then meet me on the other side of Matthew 14:22-33 _____, Mark 6:45-52 _____, and John 6:16-21. _____

John's summary of this event is brief but impactful. In John 6:21 how long does it say it took for them to get to their destination once Jesus got in their boat?

_____

Immediately! Now that is a miracle for sure but it also reminds me that no matter where I am if Jesus is welcomed in my "boat", my situation, relationship, workplace… then, immediately I'm in the right spot - there is no spot more right then right with Jesus! He may not keep us there as He loves us too much to let us sit stale and stagnant but longs to always draw us deeper into relationship with Him, but with Him we can travel anywhere.

John also records in the beginning that the disciples are waiting for Jesus… the other gospels tell us where He was. What was Jesus doing into the night?

_____

Praying. Jesus was a man of prayer. See Matthew 26:36-46, Mark 1:35, Luke 5:16; 6:12.

Mark 6:48 tells us Jesus saw they were in serious trouble and comes walking toward them on the, ON the water! Now from John's account (Jn. 6:19) I can see that the middle of the lake is about 3 to 4 miles out! This was no quick tip toe on the water top. Jesus was full-on hiking MILES on top of the raging waves!!!

May we never doubt His enduring strength made available to us through His Spirit.
In Mark 6:48 it states Jesus' intention, what is it?

_____

What? To go past them?! He saw they were deeply troubled so why would He INTEND to go PAST them?!

How did God reveal Himself in Exodus 33:12-23 to Moses?

_____

He had His glory PASS BY.

How did God reveal Himself in 1 Kings 19:9-13 to Elijah?

_____

He passed by! There was a windstorm, an earthquake and a fire but God was in the whisper.

The disciples were sure to have known these stories so might Jesus have been trying to reveal more of just Who He truly was to them?! Might we have eyes to see and ears to hear the way He is trying to reveal more of Himself to us in situations that otherwise might easily be misunderstood at first glance. Every problem is an opportunity to see things, to do things, to think of things in a new way we may have been unable to before! Is there an area in your life that you feel God is giving you an opportunity to see Him more clearly than you ever have before?

_____

_____

_____

Recognizing Jesus in your situation is the antidote to fear if we will then trust enough to abide in Him, His presence and promises. That's how we truly LIVE.

In Matthew's gospel Peter asks in 14:28, Lord, if it's really you... So Peter is not yet convinced it is. What does Peter want God to ask him to do if it truly is the Lord?

_____

Call him out! And Jesus does because He wants us ALL to have wave-walkin' faith!

The moment Peter takes his eyes off Jesus and puts them on his overwhelming circumstances what happens (Matt. 14:30)?

_____

He begins to sink.

What advice does Hebrews 12:2 give us on focus?

_____

Keep our eyes on Jesus, He is the perfecter of our faith! We can't focus on all our inadequacies if we are fixed on the great I AM.

When Jesus approaches the boat in Matthew 14:27 He says "Take courage. I am here!" (NLT) TAKE courage. Take courage I AM here. He has all the courage we need but won't force us to take it. We have to make that choice to take His courage, to receive His peace.

How can we do that? By knowing the character of I AM through prayer and His Word. In Exodus 3:14 He revealed Himself to be I AM. There is nothing He cannot be, He is I AM all that is good! Again we see Jesus pointing them back to remember what they already knew, like the story of His faithfulness to Moses and Elijah and His revealing of Himself as I AM to the Israelites in the past to embolden their faith in the present. Let's not forget to take what we remember and apply the implications to our present.

What are some things you can recall in your past that prove His faithfulness in your life? How does that embolden your faith in the present?

_____

_____

_____

_____

What does Peter cry out when he begins to sink (Matt. 14:30)?

_____

Super short prayer but it seems he is now sure about just Who is on the water with him! Before in verse 28 Peter is saying "Lord, if it's really you…" by verse 30 after his step of faith he is shouting "…LORD!"

When Peter's faith falters we need not consider it a failure as He called out to the Lord. When our faith begins to falter we too must cry out to the One, the Rock, our firm foundation that can steady us once again. And Jesus did that for Peter, not after a while, but IMMEDIATELY!!

… *"I do believe; help me overcome my unbelief!"* Mark 9:24 (NIV)

As a result of this storm what did the disciples come to know according to Matthew 14:33?

_____

You REALLY are the Son of God!

Sometimes it takes a storm of strong winds, frightening waves and a bit of sinking successes to get us to a deeper understanding of who He REALLY is!

Before we close today let's give ourselves some time to dry off and head over to Matthew 14:34-36 _____ and Mark 6:53-56. _____

These two passages tell us of the multitudes that were welcomed by Jesus. How do these passages describe these people?

_____

Sick. The sick that recognized their need for Him. He turned no one away, no one. All who touched Him were healed the text says.

Life as God has warned us can come at us in 3D, in demons, death and disease but we have the great I AM who has overcome it all and provides enduring strength. Strength to endure the unfair brokenness of this world until we reach our true and eternal Home in Paradise.

Dear one, He came to seek and save the lost (Luke 19:10), to make new from the inside out (2 Cor. 5:17).

Like Peter we can call out without hesitation. *From the ends of the earth I call to you, I call as my heart grows faint; lead me to the rock that is higher than I.* Psalm 61:2 (NIV) And like He did for Peter, God will reach out without hesitation and scoop you up into the enduring strength of His arms because... His hope does not disappoint and He just loves you.

Please record the impact to your heart today and thank you for your diligence in study this week.

_____

_____

_____

_____

Day 6 & 7: At His Feet - A Time to Reflect

Over the next two days take time to reflect over your week of study. Maybe you need some time to catch up on the study material and this might be the perfect break to do just that with the Lord!

I encourage you to glance back at the final point at the end of each day that you recorded having had the greatest impact on your heart. As you spend time with God in prayer, reflect and record on the lines below how God is tying it all together and applying it to your life.

Ask that God make it clear who He would have you invite into a natural opportunity to share Him, to apply what you are learning. Trust Him to continue to take the lead. May we have a heart ever ready with eyes and ears out to the opportunities God wants to invite us into for His glory and praise.

Do not merely listen to the word, and so deceive yourselves. Do what it says. Anyone who listens to the word but does not do what it says is like someone who looks at his face in a mirror and, after looking at himself, goes away and immediately forgets what he looks like. But whoever looks intently into the perfect law that gives freedom, and continues in it - not forgetting what they have heard, but doing it - they will be blessed in what they do.
James 1:22-25 (NIV)

_____

_____

_____

_____

Philippians 4:13 (NIV) *I can do all things through him who gives me strength.*
John 14:26 (NIV) *But the Advocate, the Holy Spirit, whom the Father will send in my name, will teach you all things and will remind you of everything I have said to you.*

WEEK 5

Jesus replied, "I am the bread of life. Whoever comes to me will never be hungry again. Whoever believes in me will never be thirsty. John 6:35 (NLT)

Day 1: The Best Quest

Welcome back my friend! We are embarking on what will begin month two of an in depth bible study! Do you feel like your heart has been driven to greater depths within your Heavenly Father's heart like I do?!

I pray that your hearts will be flooded with light so that you can understand the confident hope he has given to those he called - his holy people who are his rich and glorious inheritance. Ephesians 1:18 (NLT)

After spending a moment bowed before our Father asking that He lead us into a deeper understanding of the confident hope we have as we bask in the Truthful Light of His Word please meet me on the other side of the Scripture listed below.

John 6:22-34 _____

What question is asked by the people in verse 25?

_____

When did you get here?

To which Jesus replies directly to the heart of the motive behind that question. Jesus doesn't say, oh well I've been here about 30 minutes wondering where you were! No, Jesus answers their question about when He arrived by addressing their motive for even looking for Him. What does He say in verse 26 in response to their question?

_____

Have you ever realized you were seeking God more for what you thought He could DO for you rather than who He IS to you?

_____

It would be kind of like a child asking a parent for money to go to the movies before making genuine conversation and asking how their day was going. In a good relationship there flows good communication and through that genuine communication and mutual concern for one another, hearts are shared. The parent in this scenario would know the child's desire to attend the movie with friends and the child would not even have to ask because in the general flow of the conversation the parent would naturally sense and meet the need of their child as an outpouring of their give and take relationship.

Now we cannot give to God that which He needs, He has it all but He desires a willing relationship on our part and we can offer that to Him. Might we ask Him today to stir up a craving for more of who He is for just who He is and longs to be to us in a loving relationship rather than always going to Him because we have a "Daddy do list".

John 6:27 tells us not to be so concerned with what types of things?

_____

What should consume or drive us rather than earthly perishable things?

_____

Please read 1 Chronicles 16:11 and Matthew 6:33 and list what we are to seek.

_____

Matthew 6:31-32 tells us why we can let go of seeking our worries and just seek Him. What can you seek in Him that would lift your eyes from your worries?

_____

_____

Our Heavenly Father already knows our needs and just how to meet them ALL and even promises to do so (Phil. 4:19). So we can abide in His love, in His trustworthy promises given to us in His Word and recalled to our hearts through the Holy Spirit and prayer as we just enjoy Him.

Between John 6:28 and verse 30 there are two more questions asked by the people. The first is, what can we do? And the second is, what can You do?

In response to the first question what does Jesus say He wants us to do according to verse 29?

_____

BELIEVE. That's it, so why do we try and make it so over complicated?! I think so often we feel we need to be validated by our own works. For example, to get something we feel we need to have earned it. However we never could have earned what Jesus holds out to us. That's why He sacrificed Himself in our place - it was the ONLY way. Now the ONLY way for us to enter into eternal life is to BELIEVE in Him as our Savior. (John 14:6, John 3:16)

In response to the second question, what can You do? Jesus is aware that the Jewish people believed that when the Messiah appeared He would duplicate the same miracle that Moses performed in bringing manna from heaven. (Ex. 16) To which Jesus uses this opportunity to set the record straight. What does He say in John 6:32 to clarify just Who sent the manna back in Exodus?

_____

According to verse 33 Who is the true bread come down from heaven?

_____

How often do we look for a repeat, expecting God to work in a duplicate way as He did before or like He did for someone else when God want's to blow our minds with something new taking us totally out of our box like thinking?! How does the crowd respond now in verse 34?

_____

Give us this bread everyday! Doesn't this remind you of the women at the well's response when Jesus told her about the living water (John 4:14-15)?!!

Have you too received a spiritual awakening as you have uncovered new Truths in His Word? Explain.

_____

_____

_____

_____

Our best quest will always be for more of Him. Thank you for your time today spent in His Word. Please record below what impacted your heart the most.

_____

_____

_____

_____

Dear Heavenly Father, please give us more of You, In Jesus name - Amen.

Day 2: All Sufficient Sustenance

Welcome back to the quest for more of our good God my friend! Please begin in prayer before we jump right on in where we left off yesterday!

Todays reading is John 6:34-59_____ however you may want to back up and briefly skim over yesterdays reading which began in John chapter 6 at verse 22. This leads right up into todays segment.

In John 6:35 Jesus gives us an I AM... statement. Back in Exodus 3:14 God indicated His name is I AM. So as Jesus draws a clearer picture of who He is and wants to be to us He expounds using what we call I Am statements. Please fill in the blank according to John 6:35 NLT.

_Jesus replied, "I am the _____ of _____. Whoever comes to me will never be hungry again. Whoever believes in me will never be thirsty._ (bread, life)

In John 6:37-40 Jesus gives insight into His earthly mission. Please answer the questions by circling either Y for yes or N for no.

He will not reject anyone who comes to Him.

Y N

He came to do His own will.

Y N

God's will is that not one person who comes to Him gets lost.

Y N

Everyone who comes to Him will be raised up on the last day to eternal life.

Y N

(Answers: Y, N, Y, Y)

It sounds so simple, so wonderful, too good to be true right?! Yet what happens in John 6:41?!

_____

They stumble because of what they think they know, and the simplicity of it all to the point it becomes too complicated for them to receive!!

Have you ever made something more complicated than it had to be?

_____

_____

As a classroom teacher an acronym the teachers liked to remember was KISS. K.eep I.t S.uper S.imple The more complicated a lesson sometimes became or the more procedures a project had the more likely we were lose everyone along the way! However sometimes we have to learn this the hard way because we like to attach status or increased worth to things that are hard or appear complicated to achieve.

Jesus knows we are but dirt (Psalm 103:14) and made it as simple as possible to receive eternal life yet some still fall into the trap of needing to make it some complicated thing we need to achieve. But the thing is we never could have achieved it. In the garden Jesus asked three times if there could be another way but the answer was no. If there had been another way then I'm sure it would have been brought to light at that moment when the Father's heart must have been breaking with agony to watch His Son sweat blood with grief over the only way to accomplish our salvation. (Luke 22:39-46, Matt. 26:36-46)

In John 6:43 Jesus tells us to stop complaining… In verse 45 Jesus refers to the Old Testament Scriptures, Isaiah 54:13 and Jer. 31:33-34 which indicates we will all be taught by God. All who listen AND learn from God will respond positively to His message. Are we listening to His Word to learn or are we listening with ears pre tuned to what we think we want to hear, hearts hardened to anything else? How might we come more humbly before Him with ears and heart wide open to listen AND learn that which HE would have for us, avoiding the stumbling block of our own preconceived expectations?

_____

_____

_____

All your children will be taught by the LORD, and great will be their peace. Isaiah 54:13 (NIV)

John 6:53 starts out with Jesus repeating Himself. Whenever God repeats Himself we better pay attention! The NLT states verse 53 this way, *So Jesus said again, "I tell you the truth, unless you eat the flesh of the Son of Man and drink His blood, you cannot have eternal life within you.*

Circle the word "again" and underline the phrase, "I tell you the truth" in that verse above. Seems there is an urgency for us to listen and learn!

Flesh and blood seems to indicate the whole person. May we be people that consume all of Jesus, fully and completely believing in Him, allowing Him to consume all space within us.

Also a symbolism of His flesh (bread) broken on the cross for us and His blood (the juice) poured out for us on the cross are the elements used in the act of communion. Communion being a time to come to commune with Him in prayer remembering the act of the cross and all that was accomplished there for us, that we might gain strength to take up our cross, die to self, take His offer of His life and live for Him, in Him, anew.

Jesus is the Bread of Life. May we take Him as He is, our all sufficient sustenance.

Our God is the only carbohydrate of abundant energy filled life that comes calorie free! Amen! Let's feast away!

Thank you for today dear one. Please record the greatest impact to your heart today from your time in His Word.

_____

_____

_____

_____

Day 3: Un-Offended

Hello dear one, welcome. Today's Scripture passage begins with many of the disciples discussing what a hard teaching they felt they had received. It's never easy to receive "tough love" but the only kind of love worth receiving or even giving is the tough lasting kind. In a world that does "shallow" well, may we offer up in prayer tender hearts to receive the unfathomable depths of His love that He desires for us to know.

After prayer please continue from yesterdays Scripture into John 6:60-70. _____ If you need to take a moment to back up further in Scripture to regain context go right ahead.

Verse 60 explains the heart of the hearers at this point. How would you explain their disposition?

_____

confused , offended ...

Have you ever felt this way after receiving a word from the Lord? What did you do?

_____

_____

Jesus reminds them within verse 63 NLT, *Human effort accomplishes nothing.* We will not be able to come to a state of clarity on our own. Our best bet is to come before God and confess all our hurt, all that offends us, all our confusion, because He already knows and cares. Please record in your own words what each verse below encourages us with.

1 Peter 5:7

_____

Deuteronomy 29:29

_____

Jeremiah 33:3

_____

Matthew 11:6

_____

Isaiah 55:8-9

Jeremiah 29:11 (NIV) ...*I know the plans*... and right now we cannot in our finite minds conceive them from beginning to end (Ecc. 3:11) so we will need to rest in knowing The Beginning and The End. *I am the Alpha and the Omega, the First and the Last, the Beginning and the End.* Revelation 22:13 (NIV)

Sometimes we just need to trust the One who knows the plans. Our mind is only finite so getting frustrated and offended that we can't understand infinite things is not worth walking away from the faith and losing our salvation over. May we pray for ever increasing trust and the faith to be obedient.

Though he slay me, yet I will hope in him;... Job 13:15 (NIV) for ...*"What no eye has seen, what no ear has heard, and what no human mind has conceived" -- the things God has prepared for those who love him-- 1 Corinthians 2:9 (NIV)*

In closing please rest in the Truth of what He came to bring us stated in John 10:10. Set your course on a quest for more of The Bread of Life, for that is only where true abundant and satisfying life is found.

John 10:10 (NIV) *The thief comes only to steal and kill and destroy; I have come that they may have life, and have it to the full.*

Jeremiah 29:11 (NIV) *For I know the plans I have for you," declares the LORD, "plans to prosper you and not to harm you, plans to give you hope and a future.*

God bless you muchly~

Please record what made the greatest impact on your heart today.

_____

_____

_____

Day 4: Living True From The Inside Out

Welcome! I don't know about you but after the last couple days studying the Bread of Life I think I'd like to take this lesson with a side order of a freshly baked loaf - did I say loaf, I meant roll (I think) and warm out of the oven with a bit of melted butter please! As delicious as that may sound, aren't we all glad that even as that might not be possible at the moment, here and now we always have access to the Bread of Life... and He comes carb free!! Amen!

Let's begin today in prayer that we be open to all that He may want to pour into our soul.

Please read Matthew 15:1-20 _____ and Mark 7:1-23. _____

This story begins with some religious leaders coming to visit Jesus. According to Mark 7:2 what did they notice?

_____

Hmmm, not the most positive thing they could have noticed upon their arrival wouldn't you agree?! When you first happen upon a situation or circumstance or human being, what do you typically notice first? Is it positives or negatives? How might you move more toward noticing things with a grace and mercy filter?

_____

_____

Jesus is upset with these religious leaders. What does He call them in Matthew 15:7?

_____

Hypocrites.

These leaders had their thinking wrong. They thought because they were clean on the outside they were clean on the inside, such is not the case. We become hypocritical when we are more concerned with reputation than character and pay attention to others' sin while we conveniently look the other way from our own.

It seems Jesus first responds with the Word. He quotes Isaiah 29:13 in Matthew 15:8-9. What do these verses imply or state?

_____

_____

It seems their lives were living a "no" while their lips were giving a "yes". What does Matthew 5:37 and 2 Corinthians 1:18-20 tell us about living a life that matches? Our yes meaning yes and our no meaning no?

_____

_____

_____

If we are living as Christ's ambassadors then we need to reflect His honest faithfulness. All the promises God has given are yes in Jesus! He is faithful! How does your life speak an honest and authentic "Amen!" or yes, to who God is?

_____

_____

_____

Now Jesus doesn't call them hypocrites with no evidence to back up His claim. Jesus follows up His statement with hard evidence. In Mark 7:8-17 What evidence does Jesus give for their own hypocrisy?

_____

_____

The religious leaders are canceling the word of God to hand down their own tradition! (vs. 13) God's Word should always be the focus and any traditions we have should be to bring to life the Word but never trump or take the place of the Word. Can you share an example of a tradition you have that lifts up the Word of God?

_____

_____

Thirdly Jesus responds to these religious leaders by targeting the heart of the issue. In Matthew 15:10 Jesus calls the people together to both listen and hear. We might hear but are we listening and if we are listening are we truly hearing the message to our own hearts or are we too busy applying it to the lives of everybody else we know?

Matthew 15:12 tells us the disciples came to Jesus and asked Him a question, what was it?

_____

"Do you realize you offended the Pharisees by what you just said?" (NLT)

Have you ever said that to yourself?! Maybe you didn't mean to be offensive but you just were?! What does 2 Corinthians 2:14-16 tell us?

_____

_____

Our lives in Jesus carry the aroma of Him and to those that have not or refuse to accept Him as Lord and Savior we stink, we are offensive! Jesus was never intentionally offensive and neither should we be but we don't want to be in a position in which we are trying so hard not to offend someone with the Truth we believe that we are literally clearing the pathway to hell for them!

Jesus responds to this question in Matthew 15:13-14 (NLT) with, *"Every plant not planted by my heavenly Father will be uprooted, so ignore them. They are blind guides leading the blind, and if one blind person guides another, they will both fall into a ditch."*

What additional advice or encouragement along these same lines can you glean from Matthew 10:28, 1 John 4:4, Romans 8:31, and Psalm 124:2-5?

_____

_____

After Jesus rises from the grave and ascends into heaven there is much turmoil over all that continues to rage concerning the ministry of Jesus. What advice does the Pharisee named Gamaliel give to the people in Acts 5:34-39 that aligns with what Jesus states in Matthew 15:13?

_____

_____

Dear one, the work God has begun in your life WILL be completed (Philippians 1:6). No enemy or mean person can thwart God's purpose and plan (Job 42:2). He is The Way so align your walk with His and your way will be made - no doubt, all the way through to the finish (Psalm 37:4).

As Jesus called these leaders blind guides we too need to make sure we measure all teaching against the Bible. People are fallible and it is possible to know a lot about God and yet not know God at all.

Jesus finishes this portion of Scripture explaining that it's a heart issue. On a scale of 1-10 (1 being the least) how would you compare the time you spend working on or worrying about your outward appearances as opposed to the time dedicated toward righting or training your inward appearance? Circle one.

Time spent on outward appearance:

           1   2   3   4   5   6   7   8   9   10

Time spent on inward appearance:

           1   2   3   4   5   6   7   8   9   10

There is nothing wrong with working on the outward appearance unless it outranks in importance to the inward appearance. Psalm 139:23-24 is a good Scripture to pray when trying to lay open before God our inward appearance for a tune up. Please record those verses below.

_____

_____

_____

_____

As we close for today may we turn those above verses into a prayer that we are willing to allow God to conform us ever more into the genuinely beautiful image of His Son. Don't forget to record that which impacted your heart the most from your time in His Word today.

_____

_____

_____

_____

Day 5: Be Open

Hello and welcome! Today we will continue forward in our quest for more of our God to fill more of us. Please begin in prayer.

Treasures for the pocket in your heart today: *The Spirit of God has made me; the breath of the Almighty gives me life.* Job 33:4 (NIV) *But it is the spirit in a person, the breath of the Almighty, that gives them understanding.* Job 32:8 (NIV)

Please read Matthew 15:21-28 _____ and Mark 7:24-30. _____

What title does this woman call Jesus by in Matthew 15:22?

_____

Lord, Son of David. Apparently this lady believed Jesus was the Messiah.

What problem is she coming to Jesus with (vs. 22)?

_____

How does Jesus respond (vs. 23)?

_____

WHAT?! NO REPLY!! Have you ever felt you have received no reply in prayer?

_____

"No" and "wait" are both answers even if a "yes" is what we were hoping for. Silence is also an answer… maybe you already know the answer and He doesn't need to tell you again. Silence may also be for a time so that you lean in closer to hear His whisper that at first sounded like silence because you were too far away, too distracted by your own agenda. Silence may be because we need to purify our hearts and reverence just Who we are speaking with first. Please read Isaiah 1:15-20. _____

This woman in our passage today could have left the presence of Jesus in an offended huff when He appeared to give her the silent treatment but she stayed and stayed open to Him.

In Matthew 15:23 what do the disciples complain about?

_____

They want her to go away because they are bothering THEM!! She is there seeking Jesus and they are annoyed! Might there be anyone seeking Jesus and we cloud their vision of Him and maybe even turn them away because of how they are making US feel?! How might we begin to see people with God's heart so as to not become a stumbling block in peoples path to Jesus?

_____

_____

I believe it takes prayer and only in the Spirits power.
The woman could have walked off offended that no one wanted to include her but she stayed.

How does Jesus respond in verse 24?

_____

And yet again how does this women respond in verse 25?

_____

Worship?! This woman has been ignored and shunned and made to feel like she just doesn't fit in the "in" crowd and still instead of walking away offended she chooses to stay with an attitude of WORSHIP?!!!

Her daughter was sick folks, her need was GREAT. Have you ever experienced a need so great you left all offenses at the door?

_____

_____

I pray we don't wait for a need so great but that we can begin to let go of offenses to take on the image of God's Son more and more each day living in grace, mercy and love with a heart of pure worship.

After she worships you would think NOW she will get what she wants, she has done everything right! But what do we see in Matthew 15:26?

She gets called a dog! But with vision and a mind unclouded by offenses this woman is able to respond in truth. What does she say to Jesus in verse 27?

She humbly acknowledges the truth of her standing. Gentiles were called dogs in that day, quite possibly Jesus was revealing contrast in the way that He saw her. Treasured. His mission is to seek and save the lost, to be a light even to the Gentiles… to all nations!

She then proceeds with faith that Jesus, who she has already decided is the Messiah, would have the heart and provision to provide for the "dog's" too.

NOW how does Jesus respond to this woman in verse 28?

He commends her GREAT faith. Great faith indeed!

What sticks out to you the most, or emboldens your faith the most from this woman's example of un-offended and persistent faith?

She remained open to the heart of Jesus, the character she knew the Messiah would exemplify. When situations or circumstances make no sense and everyone around you would validate your taking offense how might you take a different attitude and rely on the faithful character of God depicted in His Word?

_____

_____

Dear one, it's not always easy to remain open minded and even harder sometimes to remain open hearted but He who promised is faithful (Hebrews 10:23) we can trust Him fully with both our mind and our hearts.

Please recored the point of greatest impact today.

_____

_____

_____

_____

Day 6 & 7: At His Feet - A Time to Reflect

Over the next two days take time to reflect over your week of study. Maybe you need some time to catch up on the study material and this might be the perfect break to do just that with the Lord!

I encourage you to glance back at the final point at the end of each day that you recorded having had the greatest impact on your heart. As you spend time with God in prayer, reflect and record on the lines below how God is tying it all together and applying it to your life.

Ask that God make it clear who He would have you invite into a natural opportunity to share Him, to apply what you are learning. Trust Him to continue to take the lead. May we have a heart ever ready with eyes and ears out to the opportunities God wants to invite us into for His glory and praise.

Do not merely listen to the word, and so deceive yourselves. Do what it says. Anyone who listens to the word but does not do what it says is like someone who looks at his face in a *mirror and, after looking at himself, goes away and immediately forgets what he looks like. But whoever looks intently into the perfect law that gives freedom, and continues in it - not forgetting what they have heard, but doing it - they will be blessed in what they do.* James 1:22-25 (NIV)

_____

_____

_____

_____

_____

Philippians 4:13 (NIV) *I can do all things through him who gives me strength.*
John 14:26 (NIV) *But the Advocate, the Holy Spirit, whom the Father will send in my name, will teach you all things and will remind you of everything I have said to you.*

WEEK 6

Search me, God, and know my heart; test me and know my anxious thoughts. See if there is any offensive way in me, and lead me on the way everlasting. Psalm 139:23-24 (NIV)

Day 1: Heart Surgery

Welcome to week six! I'm so very grateful for the diligent effort you have made to get this far in a study like this. I know He will honor your hearts desire to become more enraptured by His. Please begin in prayer as we press on.

Philippians 3:14 (NIV) is one to tuck in the pocket of our hearts this week: *I press on toward the goal to win the prize for which God has called me heavenward in Christ Jesus.*

Our Scripture for the day is found in Matthew 15:29-31 _____ and Mark 7:31-37. _____

Our Mark Scripture encompasses an example of one of the many people healed in our Matthew Scripture.

What words does Jesus speak in Mark 7:34?

_____

"Ephphatha!" Meaning "be opened." Jesus also used spit in this miracle healing. I wonder if the blind man was wishing some fresh water had been available nearby instead. Are we open to change, to new ideas and new ways of doing things?
Really?
God speaks in a language that can soften even the hardest heart if we are willing to remain open to receiving it.
God has a harvest of people out there that need to see Him clearly reflected and each one of us has been given gifts and talents to be able to do so. How open are we to let others use their gifts, their talents in the way God has given them to be used?

Please read Deuteronomy 30:6. Why does God want to circumcise our hearts according to this verse?

_____

To love Him and live!

Are you open to allowing God to do heart surgery on you? To fill your heart with pure motives, to soften it so much that it is extremely hard to offend, to be open to new ways He wants to move and use you and others for His glory?

Dear God, please help us to remain open to Your way, submitting our will to Your better one so that Satan cannot outsmart us (2 Cor. 2:11 NLT).

Let's close by praying Ezekiel 36:26, that we might allow open heart surgery to be performed on us by the Great Physician for our good and His glory.

I will give you a new heart and put a new spirit in you; I will remove from you your heart of stone and give you a heart of flesh. Ezekiel 36:26 (NIV)

Thank you for today.
Please record what made the most impact from your time in His Word.

_____

_____

_____

_____

Day 2: Simply Step Forward

Welcome my friend. Before we dive in today may we pray for an undivided focus, an open heart and the desire to make the most of this opportunity.

Let us tuck Ephesians 5:16 (NIV) into our hearts pocket today: *making the most of every opportunity, because the days are evil.*

Okay my friend let's meet each other on the other side of Matthew 15:32-39 _____ and Mark 8:1-10. _____

After having studied the feeding of the 5,000 in Matt. 14, what strikes you right off the bat regarding the disciples confusion at how the 4,000 will be provided for in today's text?

_____

_____

The disciples had witnessed Jesus feed 5,000 people with just 5 loaves and 2 fish; a young boy's single lunch leaving 12 basket fulls left over and yet they still were at a loss and worried how this need, even smaller than the first, would be met?!

As incredulous as this sounds how often can we look at our own lives and see almost identical attitudes?! We can recount and remember His faithfulness in our past and yet we still wonder and fret about our present or future concerns!!

I have always admired God's commendation of Caleb in Numbers 14:24 (NLT), *But my servant Caleb has a different attitude than the others have.* I would like to insert my own name for Caleb's however it's not that simple. To take up that different attitude, that kind of wholehearted devotion, requires an intentional trust and act of faith on my part. See in Numbers all the Israelites had been given the go ahead to invade with success the enemies land however after seeing the odds stacked against them the people trembled in fear - but not Caleb, he was determined to fix his heart, mind and spiritual eyes on his God rather than the wind and the waves of his current circumstance. He wanted to walk on water with his God and so he placed his anchor of hope in the God he knew had been faithful in the past and would be faithful now!

Do you trust that God knows what you need and cares for you?

_____

Do you trust His promise and way to provide for you?

_____

Looking back at our main text for today it was Jesus Himself that recognized and was moved with compassion for the people's needs, no one had to come report their needs to Him. It was Jesus who saw in the midst of the crowd the details of a few that had come long distances and understood as well as cared that the strain on them would be extreme to travel without food.

Matthew 6:8 tells us God knows our needs too. What need do you have right now that just knowing Jesus is aware of it brings comfort that you have not been overlooked but that He is working even now in it?

_____

_____

Might we turn that into a praise before we even know or understand how He will work it out. 2 Chronicles 20 is an example of a battle won via praise. In all that we do not know we know in the end our King has won the battle for us and stands victorious so we can praise Him that our current battle will not have the best of us. Before continuing let's turn 2 Chronicles 20:12 and Proverbs 3:5-6 into a personal prayer.

_____

_____

_____

I find it interesting that the feeding of the 5,000 was for a Jewish audience where now the feeding of the 4,000 is for a Gentile audience thus showing Himself to truly be the Bread of Life for the entire world!

Matthew 15:33 finds the disciples asking what question?

_____

Matthew 15:34 finds Jesus responding with what question?

_____

How much bread do you have? Jesus shifts their focus with His question from what they DON'T have to what they DO have.

How often do we place our focus on how much Bread we DO have rather than on our own lack apart from Him? How much of our will is submitted to trusting His better one? To the degree we have emptied ourselves is the degree to which we can be filled up with the sustaining Bread of Life, our steadfast Living Hope.

How much did they have (verse 34)?

_____

Seven loaves... seven being the number of completion. Can you imagine what God could do through a person completely emptied of self and completely filled up with Him?!! Well, nothing short of the impossible that's what! In Mark's rendition (8:1-10) I see 7 steps beginning in verse 6 following the disciples response of how much bread they have:

1. Jesus asks everyone to do what (vs. 6)?

    _____

    Sit down - What similar advice does Psalm 46:10 give us?

    _____

    So often we want to do, do, do when all He wants us to do is BE OBEDIENT. God help us to just "do" obedience. In all that you may want to do right now what does God want you to do? If you're not sure maybe it's just to abide in Him, to "sit down" and spend more time in prayer and in His Word until it becomes clear. If we walk with Him completely surrendered in our heart He will be faithful to make sure we do not miss when/if our physical feet need to move.

2. Jesus took what they had (vs. 6). He did not make comments of disbelief that it was so little. No, He received what they offered because your little in His hand will always be enough. Your weakness will never be too strong for His strength dear one.

3. Jesus thanked His Heavenly Father (vs.6). He thanked God even though it was 7 loaves for 4,000 people! What does Philippians 4:4 tell us, even repeat for us in the same verse as it is not the easiest concept to grasp or live out.

    _____

4. Jesus broke the bread into pieces (vs. 6). 2 Cor. 4:7 tells us our bodies are like jars of clay that hold incredible treasure, an all surpassing power which is the Holy Spirit. In Judges 7 a battle is won through broken jars! The jars were broken and the light from the torches within frightened the enemy so much they were overcome against all odds! Don't let the enemy outwit you, telling you you're just an old broken clay jar. Remember our God wins battles with broken clay jars so don't be afraid to beat back the enemy with the Light within you dear one!!

5. Jesus took the little the disciples had and were willing to offer Him and then Jesus blessed it and gave it back but what had changed (vs.6)?! Hint: See step 6.

6. The disciples took back from His hands and distributed to the crowd. How big was the crowd again?

    _____

    Wait.. how much had they given Jesus? All that they had, which was how much? _____ and the crowd was how much again!?!! _____ God's math always involves multiplication, He never comes up short! 7 loaves and a few small fish, all that I have + a willingness to place it ALL in His hand = a meal for 4,000 with remainders!! Eph. 3:20 tells us He is a God above and beyond what we could ever ask or imagine! We get hung up when we pre-create a frame in which we want our miracle to fit in. If God is going to bust out of the box in our mind we might as well let Him frame it too! Trust His Faithful, True and Good character of sincere and genuine love, to always be sufficient. Mark 8:8 (NLT) *They ate as much as they wanted...*

7. Verse 8 cont. (NLT) *...Afterward, the disciples picked up seven large baskets of leftover food.* Remember the number 7 is the number of completion, with seven baskets left over that looks to me like a complete example of His abundant sufficiency! In all that we lack He is more than enough.

The disciples had seen the feeding of the 5,000 and had known the Old Testament story of how God provided manna from heaven and yet in this setting they were clueless. YET Jesus still was willing to use the little faith they had to feed the hungry. What "little" do you have that Jesus could use to feed the "hungry" in your sphere of influence? Keep your heart and mind open as you ask Him to speak to you in this area coupled with a willingness to follow however He leads.

_____

_____

Please close today recording how God impacted your heart the most during your time in His Word today.

_____

_____

_____

_____

Day 3: Remember and Apply

Welcome! I cannot say enough each time you return how grateful and truly blessed I am by your diligence to continue pressing on deeper in your faith. *When we get together, I want to encourage you in your faith, but I also want to be encouraged by yours.* Romans 1:12 (NLT) Let's begin in prayer thanking God for one another as we bow our hearts to His leadership.

Please join me on the other side of Matthew 16:1-4 _____ and Mark 8:11-13. _____

The Pharisees and Sadducees were leaders in the Jewish faith however they did not see eye to eye on many religious issues. For example the Pharisees believed in the resurrection of the dead however the Sadducees did not. As different as these two parties could be they united on their dislike of Jesus.

What were these people demanding from Jesus in Matthew 16:1?

_____

A miracle doesn't convince a skeptic. A heart that chooses to be hard is just that, hard. Jesus had been healing people, feeding the thousands and still people wanted more signs! There are times in Scripture when signs were acceptable as a request to embolden faith and confirm God's voice (Judges 6:36-40) however in this situation a request for a sign was simply an obstinate testing, they had already made up their minds NOT to believe so additional signs and wonders would only fuel their excuses as to why it was not something they could accept as enough.

What does Jesus say in John 20:29?

_____

Today we have the fulfilled Word of God and years and years of church history, those that do not believe are either too stubborn or too proud. For it is only in turning to Jesus that the veil can be removed.

But whenever anyone turns to the Lord, the veil is taken away. 2 Corinthians 3:16 (NIV)

How sad for pride to be the reason we spend eternity away from our God who loved us enough to give His life in our place to pay our way.

Today in all that we may not understand might we give simply stepping forward into Him a chance. We may have fought every other way, made every other excuse, but have we tried letting our guard down in God long enough to let Him love us; to remove the veil from our eyes and heart and to simply just believe?! Believe that we could do nothing to earn His love or eternity in paradise, we just simply need to receive Him and not witness another sign or see another miracle. We already got the biggest miracle - God Almighty emptied Himself and offered Himself on our behalf that we might simply believe and LIVE!

Before moving forward please take a moment to savor the fiercely gentle humble strength of our God depicted in Philippians 2:5-11. ____

When you have all the authority to unleash all power but use it to withhold it instead, true strength is exemplified.

Let us step forward my friend to our last segment of Scripture for today. Matthew 16:5-12 _____ and Mark 8:14-21. _____

What does Matthew 16:7 say the reason is the disciples were arguing?

_____

They began to argue with each other because they hadn't brought any BREAD. When we leave the Bread of Life out of our relationships we can count on an undue amount of arguing! What does James 3:14-18 have to say about the contrast between earthly and heavenly wisdom?

_____

_____

_____

Yeast is put into bread to make it rise and only a little bit is needed. Jesus is warning them about the deceptive teaching of the Pharisees and Sadducees. Yeast is a small, very small ingredient but with big effects. We need to heed the warning in thinking some sin that seems small or a big sin done only one time is not harmful. Sin, no matter how big or small or how often or not it is engaged in will always have a negative effect on you and those around you. Do not be outwitted by the enemy!

Mark 8:14-21 lists in my NIV, 8 questions from Jesus. What are they?

1.)

_____

2.)

_____

3.)

_____

4.)

_____

5.)

_____

6.)

_____

7.)

_____

8.)

_____

As you self reflect on these questions does one question resonate with you more than the others at this point in your life today?

_____

_____

_____

- Why do we argue about not enough Bread when we can have as much as we need (Jeremiah 29:13)?

- Why do we fret about not knowing or understanding when He says He will teach us great and unsearchable things we do not yet know (Jer. 33:3)?

- If our hearts are too hard why have we not taken them to the Great Physician to trade it out for a heart of flesh (Ez. 36:26)?

- Matt. 13:16 can be our prayer for eyes and ears that truly perceive Him.

- Having trouble remembering... ask the Holy Spirit who promises to remind you (John 14:26).

- We are not to fear. Our God is the Source of all re-sources - He can not run out, He is a God of abundantly more than we could even ask for and He promises to provide for us all we need (Eph. 3:20, Phil. 4:19).

The disciples may not have failed to have remembered as much as they seemed to have missed the implications of what they remembered had on their current situation.

Today what are you remembering that is emboldening your faith for right now?

_____

_____

Don't concern yourself with tomorrow that day has enough trouble of its own (Matt. 6:34), throw that bag back on the shelf and deal with the present which is a gift for right now. None of us is guaranteed the next moment let alone tomorrow so let's take it one day at a time… with joy. Please record Psalm 118:24 below.

_____

_____

Dear one, might we pray for strength today to just simply step forward. Letting go of silly, stubborn, pride so that our hand is open to take hold of the Hand that promises to take hold of ours and help us (Is. 41:13).

Matthew 6:34 (NIV) *Therefore do not worry about tomorrow, for tomorrow will worry about itself. Each day has enough trouble of its own.*

Isaiah 41:13 (NIV) *For I am the LORD your God who takes hold of your right hand and says to you, Do not fear; I will help you.*

Please record that which held the greatest impact on your heart today.

_____

_____

_____

_____

Day 4: From Then On...

Hello. Today we will come to a turning point of sorts. Like in school around 4th grade or so you begin reading to learn instead of learning to read. The disciples will reach a point in their learning where they begin to stretch their wings but no sooner will they begin to feel the wind against their feathers than will they come to know it's God behind the wind, their wings and the thought of even flight!

John 1:3 and Colossians 1:16 are both verses to tuck into our hearts pocket. *Through him all things were made; without him nothing was made that has been made.* John 1:3 (NIV) *For in him all things were created: things in heaven and on earth, visible and invisible, whether thrones or powers or rulers or authorities; all things have been created through him and for him.* Colossians 1:16 (NIV)

After beginning in prayer please meet me over Mark 8:22-26. _____

Does it touch your heart too that Jesus takes the man by his hand and leads him outside of the village away from all the hustle and bustle (vs. 23)? Isaiah 41:13 tells us He will take us by the hand and help us too. How are you allowing Him to take your hand? How are you trusting things into His hand and allowing His comfort and strength through His trustworthy Word to help you?

_____

_____

Outside the village Jesus spits on the man's eyes (receiving help is not always comfortable), lay's His hands on the man's eyes and asks him what question in verse 23?

_____

There had always been things to see, Jesus was asking if now the man could see what had always been there to see.

The more time we spend with God away from the rush of this world; the more we allow His healing way to work in us, the more aware of His work and ways we will be. John 5:17 tells us He is always working and Matt. 13:16 says blessed are our eyes and ears if we can perceive Him.

In verse 24 the man answers Jesus that yes he can see now which is a miracle because before he had been blind! But how is he perceiving things?

_____

The people look like trees!
Jesus lays His hands on him a second time and the man's sight was completely restored (verse 25). I can interpret this in two ways. One, my perception of others and my situation and circumstances will improve, conforming more to His clearer perspective the more time I spend with God.

On the other hand if people around you look like trees maybe remember just as I am needing more time with Him to work on my perspective, He is also working with others on their "tree-like" issues as well. So maybe a bit more understanding and grace would be welcome from all angles because we probably look like a gnarly, sappy, prickly walking twig to someone else too! By His grace we are all works in progress!

Now get ready for the turning point I was speaking of earlier. Please read Matthew 16:13-20 _____, Mark 8:27-30 _____ and Luke 9:18-21. _____

In Mark 8:27 What question does Jesus ask the disciples?

_____

They answer this with the various rumors going around. They were in Caesarea Philippi, a city known for its idol worship. What a fitting place for Jesus to ask His men if they recognized Him, if they recognized Truth amidst all the lies. How good are we at deciphering Truth in this world full of lies?

_____

_____

Jesus brings it in much closer to home when He asks, *"Who do you say I am?"* in Mark 8:29 (NIV). This same question raised by the disciples in Mark 4:41 (NIV) *"Who is this?"* is answered now by one of them! Dear one, one day all that is unclear will be made clear to us too (1 Cor. 13:12).

In your city, home, school, family, that may look very much like Caesarea Philippi, do you bring a noticeable contrast? Do others recognize Him in you? How might you bring a more noticeable contrast in your sphere of influence? Or how might you encourage someone else to become bolder in the confident hope they have in Jesus?

_____

_____

Record Peter's response (Mark 8:29) to Jesus' question in that same verse (29) below.

_____

Are you convinced of this Truth? It is not enough to know what others say about Jesus, you must accept His Truth for yourself. Please write Romans 10:9 on the lines below.

_____

_____

What does Matthew 16:17 tell us about how Peter came to this revelation?

_____

Are we open to receiving new revelations from our Heavenly Father?

Later on how does Acts 4:13 describe Peter?

Unschooled and ordinary BUT it was obvious they had spent time with Jesus. Regardless of who you are or your background, upbringing or training it is time spent with an open heart before Jesus that will make the ultimate difference in your life and to those around you.

Matthew 16:21 (NLT) begins, *From then on...* there was still much for Jesus to explain and teach His disciples but from that moment on when they had accepted that He was the Messiah He begins to take them deeper into the purpose of His mission and theirs on earth.
From then on... Jesus could take them deeper into His Truths once they had accepted Him as God's Son. Look at 2 Corinthians 5:16. This verse too in the NIV starts *"from now on..."*. Explain below what information you find out in the preceding verse (2 Cor. 5:15).

Wow right! Once we have accepted the Truth that Christ died and rose again for us... from that point on we live differently! We want to live for Him rather than self when we realize just Who He is! So according to 2 Cor. 5:16 how does this change our view of others?

We begin to see others with His eyes. We begin to see others potential in Him!

1 Peter 2:2-3 (NIV) *Like newborn babies, crave pure spiritual milk, so that by it you may grow up in your salvation, now that you have tasted that the Lord is good.*

"...crave pure spiritual milk..." Keep growing in your faith, keep learning through each life circumstance allowing God to use it to reveal more of who He is and wants to be to you so from each event in your life you can look back and say, "from then on... I knew Him as... or I trusted Him to be... I found out He is..." as you continue to ever root down and grow up into Him you will flower like you never would have believed and those around you may just look a whole lot rosier too!

Thank you dear one for your diligent study of His Word today. Please record that which had the greatest impact on your heart.

_____

_____

_____

_____

Day 5: Point of View Importance

Hello! Let's jump right in without delay. First let's pray. I was greatly encouraged when my mom told me that prayer is like holding God's hand. There is peace in just holding the Hand that holds you.

Please meet me on the other side of Matthew 16:21-28 _____, Mark 8:31-9:1 _____ and Luke 9:22-27. _____

Remember back in Luke 9:18 at the beginning of all this before Jesus even brought up the discussion with His disciples as to who they thought He was as we discussed yesterday, what was Jesus recorded doing?

_____

This was a climatic event in Jesus ministry and He was prepared because He had started in prayer. Our God knows what each day holds for us. He knows all our climatic moments and wants to equip us for it all but how much time are we giving to Him in order to receive His equipping each day?

How can you develop a routine in this season of your life to best spend time with Him each day and maybe you have, or are, as you have gotten to day 5 in week 6 of this study and I'd say that is a pretty amazing start! Remember it's never too late to start, maybe look around for someone that could use some encouragement in this area.

As Jesus began to speak openly with His disciples about what was to come Mark's gospel records Peter once again speaking up. What was Peter's take on what Jesus told them concerning His suffering (Mark 8:32)?

_____

To which Jesus responds to Peter how in verse 33?

_____

Good golly! In a moment Peter went from delivering a blessed heavenly revealing to being a messenger of Satan! 1 Corinthians 10:12 (NIV) warns us all, *So, if you think you are standing firm, be careful that you don't fall!*

Peter had not been considering God's viewpoint and mission but rather his own personal thoughts and feelings. If we are not intentionally taking on the mind of Christ we too will fall into the same trap! This is one reason prayer is so very important.

The disciples job was not to guide and protect Jesus but to follow Him and such it is with us. Our job is to love God and others (Mark 12:30-31), how?... through trust and faithful obedience to Him by His Word. This is carrying your cross. Losing our self-centered determination to be in charge we would find that in dying to self we find true and abundant life in Christ.

Jim Elliot said it well, "He is no fool who gives what he cannot keep to gain what he cannot lose."

Let's close today in prayer asking that from this moment on, God give us a submissive will to His. Remaining open to His way that we might receive sight to see things from His perspective rather than merely from our own finite human viewpoint. May He stir a craving for purely more of Him in our lives.

His will is all sustaining and He works in us to energize and accomplish all He has planned for and purposed with our lives (Phil 2:13, Col. 1:29). Let's crave nothing more than the Bread of Life; take Him in and truly LIVE!

Please record the point of greatest impact today.

_____
_____
_____
_____

Day 6 & 7: At His Feet - A Time to Reflect

Over the next two days take time to reflect over your week of study. Maybe you need some time to catch up on the study material and this might be the perfect break to do just that with the Lord!

I encourage you to glance back at the final point at the end of each day that you recorded having had the greatest impact on your heart. As you spend time with God in prayer, reflect and record on the lines below how God is tying it all together and applying it to your life.

Ask that God make it clear who He would have you invite into a natural opportunity to share Him, to apply what you are learning. Trust Him to continue to take the lead. May we have a heart ever ready with eyes and ears out to the opportunities God wants to invite us into for His glory and praise.

Do not merely listen to the word, and so deceive yourselves. Do what it says. Anyone who listens to the word but does not do what it says is like someone who looks at his face in a mirror and, after looking at himself, goes away and immediately forgets what he looks like. But whoever looks intently into the perfect law that gives freedom, and continues in it - not forgetting what they have heard, but doing it - they will be blessed in what they do.
James 1:22-25 (NIV)

_____

_____

_____

_____

_____

Philippians 4:13 (NIV) *I can do all things through him who gives me strength.*
John 14:26 (NIV) *But the Advocate, the Holy Spirit, whom the Father will send in my name, will teach you all things and will remind you of everything I have said to you.*

WEEK 7

Make the most of every opportunity in these evil days. Ephesians 5:16 (NLT)…As slaves of Christ, do the will of God with all your heart. Work with enthusiasm, as though you were working for the Lord rather than for people. Remember that the Lord will reward each one of us for the good we do… Ephesians 6:6-8 (NLT) Do everything without complaining or arguing, so that no one can criticize you. Live clean, innocent lives as children of God, shining like bright lights in a world full of crooked and perverse people. Hold firmly to the word of life; then, on the day of Christ's return, I will be proud that I did not run the race in vain and that my work was not useless. Philippians 2:14-16 (NLT)

Day 1: On the Mountain

I'm so glad you came today. You are welcome here. Please bow with me in prayer that His Spirit lead in us this week making the most of our time in His Word together.

Please read Matthew 17:1-13 _____, Mark 9:2-13 _____ and Luke 9:28-36. _____

Which three disciples did Jesus bring with Him up this mountain?

_____

These three men were often in the inner circle of the circle of 12 disciples. Remember in Luke 8:51 when Jesus healed the little girl and had asked everyone to leave but Peter, James and John along with the little girl's mother and father? Maybe they had hearts ready to receive these things at the time, maybe their hearts would need these extra experiences for things in their future?! Only God knows why He gives or allows certain lives specific experiences. All we know is if He calls us up/out we best follow!

On this day not too long after Peter received the revelation that Jesus was the Messiah, Jesus takes Peter, James and John up a mountain with Him. Now if you were one of those three men and Jesus invited you up a mountain you might be getting excited because great things happened on mountains… Moses received the 10 commandments (Exodus 24), Elijah heard God's whisper (1 Kings 19), later we will see the great commission is also given on a mountain (Matt. 28)! Maybe the mountain you are being asked to climb in your life right now is to reveal to you just how much bigger your God is than you ever could have imagined before! Have you ever had a mountain sized challenge in which you got a fresh revelation of just who your God was as you crested it?

_____
_____
_____

...Truly I tell you, if you have faith as small as a mustard seed, you can say to this mountain , 'Move from here to there,' and it will move. Nothing will be impossible for you." Matthew 17:20 (NIV)

Then Jesus said to the disciples, "Have faith in God. I tell you the truth, you can say to this mountain, 'May you be lifted up and thrown into the sea,' and it will happen. But you must really believe it will happen and have no doubt in your heart. Mark 11:22-23 (NLT)

Record in your own words what happens on this mountain top (Mark 9:2-4)?

_____

_____

In Mark 9:5 Peter speaks up. What does he say?

_____

Verse 6 tells us he said this because he really didn't know what else to say and he was terrified! Have you ever spoken what you didn't mean out of fear, or rambled yourself into an uncomfortable corner for lack of knowing really what to say?

_____

_____

Sometimes when we don't know what to say, silence is our best option. Maybe our company is more in need of a listening ear than a flapping tongue. Scripture says the Holy Spirit will remind us of things and bring the right words we are to speak (John 14:26, Matt. 10:19) so if we are coming up blank maybe we are just to keep quiet!

In Peter's fear he brought Jesus down on the same playing field as Moses and Elijah. He offers to build a shelter for each as if they were equals. I think one thing that fuels fear is a distorted picture of our God. We make Him smaller than He is, we bring Him down to our playing field when He is in a league of His own!

This Peter is the same guy who just declared Jesus was God, the Messiah, and still fear trips him up in this way! Fear has a way of making all of us do and think things wonky and probably why the Bible often states, "Do not fear…"! He did not give us a spirit of fear so don't take it up (2 Tim. 1:7)!

What does God Almighty have to say in Matthew 17:5?

_____

_____

Even as Peter spoke God opened the heavens with His voice, affirming His love and approval of Jesus, His Son, but also giving the command to LISTEN to Him. At this Matt. 17:6 tells us the disciples fell face down on the ground! Well of course they did! When I am afraid, hitting the ground on my face before God Almighty in reverence and awe as He tenderly reminds me of how much bigger He is than the mountain I face is one good idea!

Matthew 17:7 touches my heart. Who comes over, reaches out and touches them, encouraging them to do what?

_____

When they did get up the only one they saw was who?

_____

You can stand in any situation when your heart and mind are fixed on only Jesus.

Let us remain standing on that mountain of Truth until we meet again tomorrow here. Please record what impacted your heart the most from your study today.

_____

_____

_____

_____

Day 2: Bring Your A-Game

Welcome back I can't wait to jump right into His Word together! Please bow in prayer before continuing on. Psalm 29:11 (NIV) *The Lord gives strength to his people; the Lord blesses his people with peace.* This is the God I want leading me today... and EVERY day!

Let's move to our parallel Scriptures for today. Matthew 17:14-21 _____, Mark 9:14-29 _____ and Luke 9:37-43. _____

Describe the scene Jesus and the three disciples come upon as they return down the mountain from our study yesterday, based on Mark 9:14-18?

_____

_____

_____

That last sentence in Mark 9:18 relays the father of the demon possessed boy stating, *So I asked your disciples to cast out the evil spirit, but they couldn't do it."* (NLT)

What does the father say in Mark 9:22?

_____

...Have mercy on us and help us, if you can. (NLT)

Jesus responds in verse 23 (NLT), *"What do you mean, 'If I can'?"...*

Remembering yesterdays study, could it be that just as Peter in his fear had brought Jesus down to the same playing field, so to speak, as Moses and Elijah, the father in our text today had brought Jesus down to the same playing field as the disciples that could not perform the miracle on his son?!

Fear and despair can distort our view and thinking of our God. We begin to measure our God against our big situation rather than measuring our situation against our big God.

Dear one, Surely the arm of the LORD is not too short to save, nor his ear too dull to hear. Isaiah 59:1 (NIV)

As Jesus points out it is never an issue of, can He, He always can however, will He? This is where trust is required. God knows and sees things we cannot begin to comprehend. If it is not in His will to respond in the way we have asked it is because ultimately it is not best. I pray all the time Matthew 11:6 that I might not fall away on account of how He chooses to do things because I know His way is best even when it may not feel like it. Faith is not based on feeling but on a tried and tested Cornerstone that will not be shaken and those who stand on it need not ever be stricken with panic or shaken.

Therefore, this is what the Sovereign LORD says: "Look! I am placing a foundation stone in Jerusalem, a firm and tested stone. It is a precious cornerstone that is safe to build on. Whoever believes need never be shaken. Isaiah 28:16 NLT

But the one who stands firm to the end will be saved. Matthew 24:13 (NIV)
*That one is to stick in your hearts pocket dear one.

This story ends with a miraculous healing! Mark 9:26 ends with everyone saying, "He's dead." Just like they did with Jairus' little girl in Luke 8 but then we have Mark 9:27 (NLT) *But Jesus took him by the hand and helped him to his feet, and he stood up.*

One touch from Jesus and what was dead comes back to life. One can stand back up under the hand of Jesus. Is there anything you need to give to Him, truly give to Him to touch with His healing hand, to lift up and bring back to life? He will work His best way over that which you fully give Him (Romans 8:28) because nothing is impossible for God and anything is possible if you believe.

_____

_____

Humble yourselves, therefore, under God's mighty hand, that he may lift you up in due time. Cast all your anxiety on him because he cares for you. 1 Peter 5:6-7 (NIV)

Maybe like the boy's father in this story we need to cry out an honest prayer as he did in Mark 9:24 (NLT) ... *"I do believe, but help me overcome my unbelief!"*
I will answer them before they even call to me. While they are still talking about their needs, I will go ahead and answer their prayers! Isaiah 65:24 (NLT)

Trust Him to give you His very best dear one, He always only brings His A-game.

Please record what has impacted your heart most from your time spent in His Word today.

_____

_____

_____

_____

Day 3: Not Afraid To Ask

Hi! How does the saying go?...the answer is always "no" if you don't ask... or is it the answer is always "yes" if you don't ask... either way why is there such fear in asking questions (if I may be so bold!)? With our God we should never fear asking our questions as He's already aware of them anyway. Often times our questions have answers beyond what we can comprehend even if we were plainly told! So I believe He gives us something better at times when answers would only create more unrest. In all our questions, in all we don't understand we can choose to receive His gift of peace that PASSES understanding.

As we begin in prayer please tuck this treasure into the pocket of your heart. Philippians 4:7 (NIV) *And the peace of God, which transcends all understanding, will guard your hearts and your minds in Christ Jesus.*

To conclude our study today please read Matthew 17:22-23 _____, Mark 9:30-32 _____ and Luke 9:43-45. _____

Whenever God Almighty repeats Himself we best pay attention. These Scriptures record Jesus predicting His death and resurrection.

What does Matthew 17:23 say about the disciples' disposition at that time?

_____

Filled with grief. Maybe they were not focusing on the raised from the dead part? Maybe they were not listening to the whole story? We too can get caught up in the grief of the moment losing our joy of salvation!

Record how Psalm 51:10-13 encourages your heart below and consider how you might make it a regular prayer in your life.

_____

_____

_____

There are and will be many things we do not understand just as the disciples did not quite comprehend everything even though they walked with God for three years on earth. However they still chose to trust, to believe and they were saved. I pray that all we do not yet understand does not keep us from noticing and enjoying His precious and faithful presence through it all.

According to Mark 9:32 what kept the disciples from bringing to Jesus what seemed to be troubling their hearts?

_____

Fear! They didn't understand but were afraid to ask. Why do you suppose they were afraid to ask?

_____

Have you ever been more afraid of the answer to a question more than you are afraid of actually asking the question?
I think this passage can embolden our faith to ask any question unafraid of any answer because in the end… in the ultimate end, if we are believers in Jesus, we have the "happily ever after" ending/answer.

Don't be afraid to ask God anything but then also stick around for the ultimate answer. *"The Son of Man is going to be delivered into the hands of men. They will kill him, AND after three days HE WILL RISE."* (Mark 9:31 (NIV) emphasis mine) Jesus did rise and so in Him we can rise too, every single time.

Dear one He always brings His A-game to your field but we must remember His field, His skill set, comes from nothing we could ever wrap our finite minds around. We must measure our God by His faithful Word and then measure our situation against the enormity of Who He is and promises to always be. There is no mountain He can't move or use to His glory and our good.

Please savor Psalm 44:3-8 before closing. _____

God bless you muchly~

Please record what had the greatest impact on your heart today.

_____

_____

_____

_____

Day 4: What Name Is On Your Jersey?

Hi! Have you ever seen the movie "Miracle"? It's a hockey movie from 2004. It's an inspirational movie and one of the quotes that sticks out to me the most is one from the character playing the coach. He says, "When you pull on that jersey, the name on the front is more important than the one on the back." You see, the team name is on the front, the individual players name is on the back. You'll win more games playing as a team than trying to play as a one man show. We were made to lift up His name not our own. The Creator of the universe has our name inscribed on the palm of His nail scarred hand (Is. 49:16) and as believers, our names are also written down in His book of Life (Luke 10:20) - that's more than enough fame for a human!

As we begin let's pray that our study today lifts up His name. *And I, when I am lifted up from the earth, will draw all people to myself."* John 12:32 (NIV) Oh, and how we want to be drawn in!

Please begin in Matthew 17:24-27. _____

Who did the collectors of the temple tax come to in verse 24?

_____

So Peter walked with Jesus closely enough that others took notice and came to ask Peter questions about Him. Is your walk close enough or consistent enough with Jesus that others take notice? Are you approachable enough that if they have a question about Jesus you would be someone they could ask? What qualities about someone makes YOU comfortable asking them questions about anything?

_____

_____

In verse 25 Peter answers but maybe before he really knows the correct answer because Jesus brings a lesson up here. It is important that whether we think we know or we think we don't we always double check with the One who does before going ahead in word, thought or action.

Jesus uses this situation to emphasize His Kingly role. Amazing how Jesus can use even the times we misstep/misspeak for good. Just as kings paid no taxes and collected none from their family, Jesus THE King was exempt from paying temple tax. However as not to offend those that did not understand His Kingship He paid the tax.

How did Jesus pay this tax?

_____

Peter had to GO - OPEN - TAKE - Go down to the lake, catch a fish, open the mouth of the first fish he caught and TRUST that what he needed would be there!!

Everything we have comes from God but He may ask us to play a part, an active part in the process. How do we do this? Cling to the promises in His Word. Glance at Genesis 6:17-18 and verse 20. _____

The temptation is to get so wrapped up in the negative that we never catch the positive promise. If Noah had lost his mind in verse 17 he would have missed the "But" in verse 18 and that important piece of information tucked in verse 20 about being "kept alive"!

We see Jesus yet again exemplify this perfect trust in John 16:12-13 and since we are there glance also at verse 32. _____

Jesus had much more to tell his men but they were not ready to receive it. Jesus had the cross right around the corner, rather than freak out about so little time and so much to do He gave us the "but" in verse 13. Jesus would need to take the cross, rise again and return to heaven BUT we would not be left alone for the Spirit of Truth would be given to us as believers. Jesus was confident the gift of the Holy Spirit would be more than enough to carry us through all the way to where He was going! If Jesus was that confident in the Holy Spirit then we too should follow suit, placing our trust in Him in us as we GO - OPEN - TAKE to fulfill His purpose with our lives.

The end of verse 32 in John 16 records Jesus saying, (NIV) *You will leave me all alone. Yet I am not alone, for my Father is with me.*

You dear one are not alone! The team Name on your Jersey is the One, the ONLY One under which we are kept alive! Cling to the promises, the good and faithful promises of our God and go carry His victory into the world!

Acts 4:12 (NIV) *Salvation is found in no one else, for there is no other name under heaven given to mankind by which we must be saved."*

Please record the impact to your heart from John 15:5 and 1 Chronicles 29:14.

_____

_____

We never walk on the playing field of life alone for He has said, never will I leave you (Hebrews 13:5). The greatest gift we will ever bring to the world is the Holy Spirit within us, so go play God-confident!

Please record the point that you will remember most from your study today.

_____

_____

_____

_____

Day 5: Waiters Serve

Welcome friend. As we embark on our quest to grow stronger in Him, greater in faith and trust, I am encouraged by your tenacity to continue to come back to the water of His Word that He might grow us up into all the fullness of who He is. Growth takes time. I was reminded recently that if we are waiting on God we might as well do what waiters do… serve! What are you waiting on today that is allowing you time to serve like never before?!

Let's bow our hearts and minds to the Gardener of our souls that He might do a work in us only He could do and that as we wait may we serve.

Tuck this one in tight inside the pocket of your heart. *He answered, "Love the Lord your God with all your heart and with all your soul and with all your strength and with all your mind'; and, 'Love your neighbor as yourself.'"* Luke 10:27 (NIV)

I've heard it stated that if serving in beneath you than leading is beyond you.

Please turn and read Matthew 18:1-5 _____, Mark 9:33-37 _____ and Luke 9:46-48. _____

What is the beginning argument over?

_____

Just after Jesus predicts His death the disciples are heard arguing over who will be the greatest in God's Kingdom!! Sounds incredulous but if we can identify "it" (whatever wrong or shortcoming "it" defines: gossip, envy, selfish ambition...) more than likely we have been a part of "it" in some way ourselves.

The disciples had begun to lose sight of Jesus' divine purpose. Maybe it was because some got to go up on the mountain of transfiguration and some did not or that they were unable to get the demon out of the last father's son that came to them for help while Jesus was up on that mountain... There are many petty things that can get our vision obscured from our God ordained purpose.

Be alert and of sober mind. Your enemy the devil prowls around like a roaring lion looking for someone to devour. 1 Peter 5:8 NIV

What kind of person does Jesus use as an example to be like?

_____

A child. Jesus didn't say be childISH but rather childLIKE there is a big difference.

A child is not intent on status or ambition but rather is trusting and humble.

In Mark's gospel account Jesus states in Mark 9:35 (NLT) … *"Whoever wants to be first must take last place and be the servant of everyone else."* This could not be more opposite than the way of the world. However the best leaders are those that are servant hearted. Describe below the qualities of a leader in authority over you that you admire.

_____

_____

Have you told them lately?

Mark 9:37 finds Jesus telling everyone that whoever welcomes a child on His behalf welcomes Him and by way of Him, His Father too. This was profound because in that day children were considered inferior and weak as were women yet Jesus elevated both, placing importance on every life.

What does Matthew 18:10 have to say about the importance of children in God's sight?

_____

_____

Don't let anyone look down on you because you are young, but set an example for the believers in speech, in conduct, in love, in faith and in purity. 1 Timothy 4:12 (NIV)

Let's head over to our last group of Scriptures for today. Please read Mark 9:38-41 _____ and Luke 9:49-50. _____

What seems to be concerning the disciples now?

_____

_____

They were concerned because someone outside their group was casting out demons. How does Jesus respond according to our passages?

_____

People that truly follow Jesus will have the same goal of trying to build up His Kingdom and His Kingdom workers even if they look different than us or don't belong to all the same groups as us. Are there certain differences between believers that are causing you to get distracted from the main goal of building up His Kingdom? Are these differences core building blocks to our beliefs or are they petty differences that can be set aside to serve side by side more effectively?

READ Ephesians 2:14-16. _____

Are we more focused on personal achievement or unselfish service? Are we more concerned about His name on the front door of our heart or with our name in lights? The only team that wins in the end is team Jesus.
Jesus is "'the stone you builders rejected, which has become the cornerstone.' Salvation is found in no one else, for there is no other name under heaven given to mankind by which we must be saved." Acts 4:11-12 (NIV)

Please circle the name "Jesus" and the phrase, "no other name under heaven" in the above verse.

NO OTHER NAME. (period) The last became first. The enemy thought he had Him on the cross but the final word had not yet been spoken! Dear one, at the blow of the final whistle in this game called life we are going to want to be playing under the Name that is above every other name and that is the name, Jesus.

Please read Colossians 2:15 and Romans 16:20 and record the impact those verses have on your mind and heart.

_____

_____

Humble yourselves, therefore, under God's mighty hand, that he may lift you up in due time. 1 Peter 5:6 (NIV)

Close today savoring Philippians 2:5-11. _____

The choice is yours to wear His Jersey; you're already wanted on His team dear one, that's one spot your don't have to wait on!

Please record what made the greatest impact on your heart from today's study. Thank you for joining me!

_____

_____

_____

_____

Day 6 & 7: At His Feet - A Time to Reflect

Over the next two days take time to reflect over your week of study. Maybe you need some time to catch up on the study material and this might be the perfect break to do just that with the Lord!

I encourage you to glance back at the final point at the end of each day that you recorded having had the greatest impact on your heart. As you spend time with God in prayer, reflect and record on the lines below how God is tying it all together and applying it to your life.

Ask that God make it clear who He would have you invite into a natural opportunity to share Him, to apply what you are learning. Trust Him to continue to take the lead. May we have a heart ever ready with eyes and ears out to the opportunities God wants to invite us into for His glory and praise.

Do not merely listen to the word, and so deceive yourselves. Do what it says. Anyone who listens to the word but does not do what it says is like someone who looks at his face in a mirror and, after looking at himself, goes away and immediately forgets what he looks like. But whoever looks intently into the perfect law that gives freedom, and continues in it - not forgetting what they have heard, but doing it - they will be blessed in what they do.
James 1:22-25 (NIV)

Philippians 4:13 (NIV) *I can do all things through him who gives me strength.*
John 14:26 (NIV) *But the Advocate, the Holy Spirit, whom the Father will send in my name, will teach you all things and will remind you of everything I have said to you.*

WEEK 8

She gave this name to the LORD who spoke to her: "You are the God who sees me," for she said, "I have now seen the One who sees me." Genesis 16:13 (NIV)

Day 1: Play With Integrity

Hello my friend, welcome back. When I was a kid and my family would go out to eat at a place you had to wait for your order to arrive, my dad would do all sorts of entertaining tricks to keep myself and my many siblings entertained during the wait. One such trick was pouring a bit of salt out on the table and then miraculously balancing the salt shaker (to our awestruck amazement) on

137

just it's very edge mid air! This memory with it's thrilling crowd appeal has carried on down a generation as I now perform it for my kids in restaurants to pass the wait time in awestruck wonder!

This salty memory was brought up to the forefront of my mind as our text today uses the memory of salt to illustrate a spiritual truth. Before we dive into our study today please bow with me in prayer and ask that God Almighty season our time in His Word to delectable perfection!

Alright please meet me on the other side of Matthew 18:6-10 _____ and Mark 9:42-50. _____

These verses are not meant to be taken literally as in cutting off one's appendages but rather to paint the picture of how seriously sin should be dealt with in one's life. Sin must be cut out of one's life as it separates us from a relationship with God. No sin is worth going to hell for.

Giving up a job or relationship or activity because it goes against God's way may seem excruciatingly painful at the time but we must make our choices with an eternal perspective. Is there anything you feel needs to be cut out of your life? It may not seem to be anything big, but the cost for the big sins and the small sins was the same - Jesus paid our debt with the sacrifice of His life. There are no "small" sins in the light of such a cost. Take some time with God praying Psalm 139:23-24.

_____

_____

_____

If we confess our sins, he is faithful and just and will forgive us our sins and purify us from all unrighteousness. 1 John 1:9 (NIV) Please circle the word "all" in that verse.

Everyone will be salted with fire. Mark 9:49 (NIV) Tested with fire or salted with fire has a purifying affect just as salt itself does. Being a "salty Christian" refers to a genuine character with purifying influence.

Mark 9:50 refers to salt losing what?

_____

Flavor.

We can look like a healthy Christian on the outside but what does the flavor of the salt produced in our life taste like? Who in your life would you describe as a genuinely salty Christian? Why?

_____

_____

Have you thanked them lately for their "salty" example in Christ?

A salty Christian remembers God's faithfulness and acts from trust. In Leviticus 2:13 salt was used in sacrifice to remind people of God's covenant with them.

A salty Christian is one that brings contrast into the world. As salt makes food taste better so should a Christian elevate his environment or sphere of influence.

A salty Christian counteracts the moral decay in this world just as salt acts as a preservative to food. What good are we, how effective, in the Kingdom purpose are we when we lose our desire to love and live like Jesus?

If you feel dull pray Psalm 51:10-12. Read His Word. Jeremiah 23:29 declares His Word to be like fire! His Word is just the kind of fire we need down in our bones to make our life explode with saltiness that just cannot be contained (Jer. 20:9)!

Alright my friend are you pruning up with the water of His Word as the salt within you just makes you thirst ever more deeply for it?!! Me too and I pray the craving never ceases! Head with me over to Matthew 18:15-20. _____

Honesty and humility are characteristics of a true follower of Jesus. As we see in verse 15 the point of pointing out an offense is what?

_____

To win someone back, to fix a relationship. Sometimes in the heat of the moment it is good to pause and check the motive in our heart before pointing out faults and offenses in others. What wise advice does Matthew 7:4-5 offer us all?

_____

_____

If our motives are pure the language we speak with should be His love. What do we sound like if we don't (see 1 Corinthians 13:1)?

_____

What happens when we do speak in His love (see Ephesians 4:15)?

_____

If a person refuses to listen to you what are you to do next (Matthew 18:16)?

_____

Remember this scenario concerning confrontation encompasses another believer not someone who does not believe. Read 1 Corinthians 5:12-13 for further clarification.

According to Matthew 18:17 if the person still refuses to listen to reason you are to take your case to

_____

The church.

In 1 Corinthians 5 a case is brought to the church and verse 5 tells us why. Please state it below.

_____

So that this believer could be restored! By 2 Corinthians 2:5-11 we see that the church was successful in binding the sin, leading in correction and extending forgiveness so restoration of this man could occur.

Matthew 18:19 refers to the importance of group prayer. Within a group commitment to pray together there is more likely to be consistency. Just like going to the gym or walking daily has a higher success rate if you set a goal and commit with a friend then on your own.

One last note on reconciliation. Please read Matthew 18:21-22 (which will actually kick start our study tomorrow) and record anything God lays on your heart.

_____

_____

All Scripture is God-breathed and is useful for teaching, rebuking, correcting and training in righteousness, so that the servant of God may be thoroughly equipped for every good work. 2 Timothy 3:16-17 (NIV)

Please record what impacted your heart the most today as you studied His Word.

_____

_____

_____

_____

Day 2: To Infinity and Beyond

Greetings dear friend. I'm currently waiting for my local grocery store to be open so that I can get the grocery shopping done before school begins today. This early the store is never that crowded, things haven't been picked over, the check out lines are pretty much non existent and I get to watch the sun rise on my way home.

One of the best things about getting up (at least what seems like) before the rest of the world is that calm peaceful quietness that cleanses your mind and heart with the awareness of God's nearness. The stillness makes that much louder all the little things that usually get so easily drowned out during the hustle and bustle in the middle of the day. We can tune into the whisper of our ultimate Prince Charming... Psalm 143:8 (NIV) *Let the morning bring me word of your unfailing love, for I have put my trust in you. Show me the way I should go, for to you I entrust me life.*

Do you hear His whisper of unfailing love to your heart today dear one? I pray that you do. Nothing, no nothing could ever separate you from His love. We are forgiven and set free by the power of His blood.

Go ahead and spend time with God in prayer before we embark together today in His Word.

In him we have redemption through his blood, the forgiveness of sins, in accordance with the riches of God's grace that he lavished on us. With all wisdom and understanding. Ephesians 1:7-8 (NIV) What a wonderful verse to tuck into the pocket of our hearts today. I love that God lavished on us His grace WITH all wisdom and understanding! He knows us completely and still chooses to love us, to lavish us with grace. Oh praise Him!

Please meet me on the other side of Matthew 18:21-35. _____

How many times does Peter offer to forgive in verse 21?

_____

This suggestion from Peter would have appeared quite generous because the rabbis taught to forgive an offense up to 3 times. It would've been quite shocking to then receive the response that our willingness to forgive should be like God's! We can only forgive like God through God in us.

Romans 5:5 tells us by the Holy Spirit, God's love has been poured out in us. We can forgive and love to the level of Him in us. How much of Him in you do you have? Ephesians 3:19 reminds us that we can be filled to all the measure of all the fullness of God. What might we need to empty out of ourselves to make more room for Him to fill us to the next level?

_____

_____

Seventy times seven really means an infinite amount of forgiveness. To infinity and beyond! Forgiveness from where (see Matthew 18:35)?

_____

The heart. Forgiveness in sincerity from the heart will exemplify a change of attitude, speech, and quite possibly eye posture (you know what I mean right?! Eye glaring and rolling… those exasperated expressions and heavy sighing would definitely be left in the dust with true and sincere forgiveness). Oh and the recalling of faults would also be left out too. There is no room for that if we are trying to make more room for God's Spirit.

Just as the first debt was much higher than the second in this story so it is when we compare that God offers us forgiveness over ALL our sin over our ENTIRE lifetime, to that one person and their sin against us for a particular moment in time. For us to withhold forgiveness and love when not only has He forgiven us but has ALSO said we can use HIS love and forgiveness to give to others, who are we to withhold any forgiveness, grace and mercy that we have so readily and freely received from Him first?!

This topic is not easy and He never said it would be. It is only in Him that we can be successful at it. Praise Him that His mercy for us is new every morning - free for the taking - free for the giving.

The steadfast love of the Lord never ceases; his mercies never come to an end; they are new every morning; great is your faithfulness. Lamentations 3:22-23 (ESV)

Be kind and compassionate to one another, forgiving each other, just as in Christ God forgave you. Ephesians 4:32 (NIV)

Today let's be better not bitter. Please record what made the most impact on your heart today.

_____

_____

_____

_____

Now off to get those groceries! But more importantly I pray to be filled with God's groceries, the fruit of His Spirit as relayed in Galatians 5:22-23 - love, joy, peace, patience, kindness, goodness, faithfulness, gentleness and self-control. Dear one, let's praise Him that His groceries are always free! Let's fill up our basket, our hearts, to infinity and beyond in order to bring Him glory and praise. God bless you muchly~

Day 3: Shoot To Score

Hi. I'm just so glad you are here today. Thank you for coming. *Every time I think of you, I give thanks to my God.* Philippians 1:3 (NLT) Let's bow together in prayer that God be honored and us encouraged through our time of study today.

As we begin let's tuck Revelation 3:8 (NIV) into our hearts pocket. *I know your deeds. See, I have placed before you an open door that no one can shut. I know that you have little strength, yet you have kept my word and have not denied my name.*

Please meet me on the other side of John 7:1-9. _____

The Festival of Shelters or Feast of Booths (Deut. 16:13-15) was an event that took place in the fall about six months after the Passover celebration (Deut. 16:1-8). This was an event for the whole family to remember and teach all ages about the faithful goodness of our God. Kind of like a big family camp! What kinds of things do you do as a family to pass down, celebrate and remember the faithful goodness of our God?

_____

_____

_____

During the Festival of Shelters the, people lived in short term shelters for a week as a reminder of the tents the Israelites used for the forty years they wandered in the desert. Can you imagine tent camping for 40 years!! However Nehemiah 9:21 (NIV) reminds us that His grace is sufficient. *For forty years you sustained them in the wilderness; they lacked nothing, their clothes did not wear out nor did their feet become swollen.*

REMEMBER His sustaining and sufficient grace, celebrate it and tell the next generation of it! Not just the young but the middle aged and the old - always proclaim the good faithfulness of our God!

The one who regularly speaks His promises out-loud, sings out His praises in worship, and prays on all occasions… is a mighty God warrior the enemy can not stand against!

Check out Psalm 71:14-19 before moving on. _____

In John 7:3-5 we see Jesus' brothers reminding Him of the religious obligation to celebrate this festival yet not too kindly. Although some of His brothers became prominent leaders in the church it wasn't until after His death and resurrection that they truly believed in Him as the Messiah.

In verse 6 Jesus says it's not the right time. Why was it not the right time?

_____

The leaders were plotting His death. Jesus had more to do yet had to work not as openly as He would have probably liked due to the evil plot against Him. No one else could see the plan like He could. No one else can see the plan now like He can! Jer. 29:11 states, He knows the plans… When things don't make sense how might we gain courage to trust the One who knows, has, and understands the plans?

_____

_____

Speak out His truth, sing His praise and pray. Romans 12:2 (NIV) *Do not conform to the pattern of this world, but be transformed by the renewing of your mind. Then you will be able to test and approve what God's will is--his good, pleasing and perfect will.*

By wisdom the LORD laid the earth's foundations, by understanding he set the heavens in place; Proverbs 3:19 (NIV)

He knows what He is doing my friend, it's when we focus more on the waves rather than the Wave Walker that we get disoriented.

May we not take for granted the moments of freedom we do have to proclaim the Good News. Ephesians 5:16 (NIV) reminds us to make *the most of every opportunity, because the days are evil.* Time is short. We have one life to make an impact on the population of His Kingdom. When we get there everyone there will already know the Good News so now is our time. You don't want to get there and look to the other side and find people wishing you had bothered them one more time with the Good News and it then being too late.

You are the right age for God's agenda, I've heard it stated that God's time is your prime time... and you miss 100% of the shots you don't take, so step up today! Hebrews 10:35, 39 encourages us to step forward, to not throw away our God-confidence! Your time is now, you've one life to live! Praise our God who catches every rebound and tosses us back the ball and says, "keep shootin'!"

Please record what has impacted your heart the most from todays study.

_____
_____
_____
_____

Day 4: Authentic Change
Hello friend. I'm so excited to get started! Please pray that God take the lead as we bow our hearts and minds to His best will and way.

Change is hard for all humans I think, at least to some degree. Change produces a bit of vulnerability. Change often affords opportunity to grow, stretch and learn... all of which can be uncomfortable. We have a God who knows and understands what we are going through when we feel the strain of the change.

Please read Philippians 2:6-8. _____ What did God submit to in order to save us?

_____

_____

He moved from heaven to be born in a manger! The God beyond the limits of all time and space, allowed Himself to be confined by it within a human shell! He chose to be the sacrifice for OUR sin to change our eternal destiny! Keeping in mind all that He changed for us (that literally we cannot even really begin to wrap our minds around) please read Luke 9:51-56. _____

In verse 51 how does it state Jesus set out for Jerusalem?

_____

My NIV states, resolutely.

Why do you think He had to go with such set determination?

_____

Jesus knew He would face persecution and death and He had determined to complete His mission at all cost.

Have you ever faced something in which you had to resolutely set yourself, in order to accomplish it?

_____

_____

On Jesus' way He went through Samaria which most Jews never would have done. Samaritans were a mixed race so "pure" Jews and Samaritans found reason to not get along, to say the least. Jesus however loves all equally (Romans 2:11).

When the Samaritans did not welcome Jesus due to His destination what did James and John ask Jesus in Luke 9:54?

_____

Jesus was not too happy with their request.

What advice does Romans 12:19-21 give us?

_____

_____

Interesting isn't it, that this John who wants to call down fire on a whole group of people later writes the gospel known for it's love?!!

Walking with God submitted to His will and way is a life process of authentic life change.

Therefore, if anyone is in Christ, the new creation has come: The old has gone, the new is here! 2 Corinthians 5:17 (NIV)

Before closing please go back and read Philippians 2:1-18. Please recored your hearts response in a prayer below.

_____

_____

_____

_____

Don't give up in the cocoon. Be willing to submit to the change. You won't want to miss the butterfly He's producing through it all dear one!

Please record the greatest impact to your heart as you studied His Word today.

_____

_____

_____

_____

Day 5: Cross or Crown

Well done my friend! Thank you for choosing to make studying His Word a priority. I know you have or you never would have made it to day five in week eight of an in-depth study of His heart! Let's keep going! Beginning in prayer *for it is God who works in you to will and to act in order to fulfill his good purpose.* Philippians 2:13 (NIV)

Go ahead and tuck James 1:12 (NIV) into the pocket of your heart. *Blessed is the one who perseveres under trial because, having stood the test, that person will receive the crown of life that the Lord has promised to those who love him.*

Please read Matthew 8:18-22 _____ and Luke 9:57-62. _____

Here we see pictured under eagerness and over eagerness to follow Jesus. We don't want to follow God because He can give us all we want but rather because He is worth all we got!

The first man in Luke 9:57 tells Jesus what?

_____

To which Jesus kindly reminds him of what in verse 58?

_____

We all want such eagerness to follow Christ but measured with reality so as not to fall away when things are difficult.

If Jesus had no place to call home His disciples must expect no less. Remember this earth is just where we work for awhile, our true Home is Heaven in which you most certainly have a place!

Read John 14:3 and Hebrews 11:10 and record the encouragement it offers you.

_____

In Jesus we all have something to look forward to!

In Luke 9:59 Jesus calls another man and how does that man respond in that very same verse which is very similar to the response of the man in verse 61?

_____

Yes Lord, but first…

What does Matthew 6:33 remind us we are to seek first?

_____

Jesus is not teaching to forsake family responsibility but rather, as He often did, gave commands concerning the true motives in a heart. It is likely that if the one man's father had died he would have already been there taking care of the situation. Or, maybe he was delaying the reality of going and following Jesus, maybe he thought he needed to wait and receive the inheritance coming his way before leaving it all behind… There is a cost in following Jesus (which ends in unfathomable reward) however He is looking for those willing to serve even when self sacrifice is required. His eyes roam the earth to strengthen those wholeheartedly devoted to Him as He knows the cost is costly (2 Chronicles 16:9).

What does Jesus say in Luke 9:62?

_____

Looking back while plowing forward would cause a plow to go off course. If our eyes are placed anywhere other than God we will go off course. Faith moves forward. Don't get tripped up on your past, focus forward.

Jesus desires total dedication regardless of the cost, not a half hearted commitment, we must accept the cross and the crown. Step up to the line, take the shot... you can't score the point if you don't first toss the ball in the air and you can't score the point with a halfhearted toss. Today: cross or crown, shoot to score!

I press on toward the goal to win the prize for which God has called me heavenward in Christ Jesus. Philippians 3:14 (NIV)

Dear one, He's won the game but this set, this match is yours for such a time as this. Get on the field, play your heart out for the Name above every other name, the Name who gave it all to have yours etched in His book of life; play with His integrity poured into your heart and... shoot, cross or crown, determined to score!

Please record the greatest point of impact today. God bless you muchly~

_____
_____
_____
_____

Day 6 & 7: At His Feet - A Time to Reflect

Over the next two days take time to reflect over your week of study. Maybe you need some time to catch up on the study material and this might be the perfect break to do just that with the Lord!

I encourage you to glance back at the final point at the end of each day that you recorded having had the greatest impact on your heart. As you spend time with God in prayer, reflect and record on the lines below how God is tying it all together and applying it to your life.

Ask that God make it clear who He would have you invite into a natural opportunity to share Him, to apply what you are learning. Trust Him to continue to take the lead. May we have a heart ever ready with eyes and ears out to the opportunities God wants to invite us into for His glory and praise.

Do not merely listen to the word, and so deceive yourselves. Do what it says. Anyone who listens to the word but does not do what it says is like someone who looks at his face in a mirror and, after looking at himself, goes away and immediately forgets what he looks like. But whoever looks intently into the perfect law that gives freedom, and continues in it - not forgetting what they have heard, but doing it - they will be blessed in what they do.
James 1:22-25 (NIV)

_____

_____

_____

_____

Philippians 4:13 (NIV) *I can do all things through him who gives me strength.*
John 14:26 (NIV) *But the Advocate, the Holy Spirit, whom the Father will send in my name, will teach you all things and will remind you of everything I have said to you.*

WEEK 9

The LORD is my light and my salvation; whom shall I fear? The LORD is the stronghold of my life; of whom shall I be afraid? Psalm 27:1 (ESV)

Day 1: His Time, His Way

Hello friend. Thank you sincerely for continuing to study along side me. I praise Him as He continues to meet us where we stand and walk us forward. Let's press on just as Paul stated, press on toward the goal, to reach the end of the race for the prize, a prize that far outweighs any earthly gain (Phil. 3:14). Please bow with me yet individually in prayer before we dive into today's study. I've heard it said, you can stand before anyone, if you first kneel before The One. Prayer is like holding the hand of God. *I keep my eyes always on the LORD with him at my right hand, I will not be shaken.* Psalm 16:8 (NIV) Let us proceed allowing our God to ever steady us in Him.

Take a deep breath, settle in and just enjoy John 7:10-52. _____

Backtracking just a bit, what was Jesus' plan according to John 7:8?

_____

What happens in John 7:10?

_____

What happens about midway through the festival in John 7:14?

_____

What happens on the last day of the festival, the climax of the festival in verses 37-38? With what kind of voice does verse 37 say Jesus used?

_____

Do you too see the progression? At first Jesus says it's not the right time because He knows He is on a mission and He must be strategic in carrying it out as there were many that opposed Him.

Yet in His time He does attend the festival and midway through begins to teach and not all too secretly might I add! Where does verse 14 indicate Jesus began to teach?

_____

The Temple in the middle of festival time!

By the end of the festival Jesus is shouting His message for all the crowd to hear! What is His message? (verses 37-39)

_____
_____
_____

Jesus moved with and at the pace the Father strategically set.

Jesus could have sat down discouraged that He had to go secretly to the festival when He had a message burning in His heart that needed to be shouted to all the crowd.

He could have been disobedient thinking He knew better than the Father, after-all He was walking among the people and could clearly see they needed the living water He had to give!

What Jesus chose to do set's a deafening message to my heart. What does it speak to yours?

_____
_____

Hebrews 6:7-8 (NLT) states, *When the ground soaks up the falling rain and bears a good crop for the farmer, it has God's blessing. But if a field bears thorns and thistles, it is useless. The farmer will soon condemn that field and burn it.*

When the ground soaks up the falling rain... The rain is going to fall, what are you going to do with it? Will it erode you? Will it water distracting things in your life that will grow and choke out your God given potential and purpose?

OR... when the rains of life fall and you maybe can't go to the "festival" like you would like to, you can choose to receive the rain, the living water of God's Word, His Spirit and mature up into Him. Does the rain refine your character to trust and obey? Does the rain run deep and produce good fruit from the seed in the soil of your heart?

Jesus moved with the Father and He moved at the Father's pace. Jesus trusted the Father, and the message the Father had put in His heart to proclaim for the Kingdom got out in the Father's time, and in the Father's way, to the Father's glory and praise!

To this day we get to treasure the message that Jesus gave in John 7:37-39 because Jesus submitted once again to the Father in Heaven while He Himself walked on earth. As tempting as it might have been to reason out that He was the One in the thick of it and knew best, He instead gave us the best example of how we should live... in humble submission, trusting the One who knows best how to work out His purpose in, through and for our lives.

How can we apply this lesson through Jesus' example to our lives currently?

_____

_____

We will pick up in this same Scripture passage tomorrow. For now please record what made the greatest impact on your heart today from your time in His Word.

_____

_____

_____

_____

Day 2: Standing, Heart Open

Welcome back! I'm excited to jump back into the living water of His Word today. Please bow in prayer before beginning.

Go ahead and tuck this treasure into the pocket of your heart today dear one. Psalm 16:11 (NIV) *You make known to me the path of life; you will fill me with joy in your presence, with eternal pleasures at your right hand.*

Go ahead and refresh your mind by briefing back over the passage we began studying yesterday in John 7:10-52. _____

John 7:10-12 finds everyone arguing about just who Jesus is. Who do you say that He is? At the end of the line it will not matter what someone told you but rather what you believed for yourself was true about Him. John 14:6 tells us Jesus is the Way, Truth and Life - Belief in Who He is, as the Bible says He is, is the only way to life eternal.

John 7:13 (NLT) states, *But no one had the courage to speak _____ about him in public, for they were _____ of getting in trouble with the Jewish leaders.*
(favorably, afraid)

What does 2 Corinthians 3:12 state?

_____

_____

The degree to which you are confident in your hope is the degree to which you will be bold about sharing it.

John 7:15 tells us Jesus was questioned because He seemed to know so much yet was untrained! How does Jesus respond in verse 16?

_____

His validation and message was from God who had sent Him.

How secure are you rooted in the Truth that what God has called you to do you are fully equipped to handle in Him? His validation should be what drives you; His message in you is sufficient. You have what it takes to carry the Light He has placed in you for His glory.

As you walk with Him in His Word and in prayer seeking His face and strength continually (1 Chronicles 16:11) He will give you opportunity to grow and learn but do not be discouraged if the world can't see what is True in you, the only One that truly matters does see. *So she called the name of the LORD who spoke to her, "You are a God of seeing," for she said, "Truly here I have seen him who looks after me."* Gen. 16:13 (ESV) *For we are to God the pleasing aroma of Christ among those who are being saved and those who are perishing. To the one we are an aroma that brings death; to the other, an aroma that brings life. And who is equal to such a task?* 2 Corinthians 2:15-16 (NIV) Apart from Him none of us are equal to such a task (John 15:5).

Please read the following and record what impacts your heart.

Galatians 1:10

_____

_____

Colossians 3:23

_____

_____

Hebrews 6:10-11

_____

_____

In John 7:21-24 Jesus addresses the law they are so wrapped up and worried about, more so than the condition of their hearts. What does Deuteronomy 30:6 tell us God will graciously do for us if we will submit to Him?

_____

_____

A circumcised heart will enable us to carry out John 7:24. Please write verse 24 out below.

_____

_____

This verse could become a daily prayer.

I don't believe any of us would be willing to hand God Almighty the stick with which we so often measure/judge others and say, "sure God use my stick to measure me in the final judgment rather than Yours."

A bit more grace and a bit more mercy (and sometimes a whole lotta "bit") would do us all a world of good or the whole world good!

In John 7:27 the people wonder how Jesus could be the Messiah. The very next sentence in my NLT in verse 27 is, For we know… How often does what we THINK we know become our biggest stumbling block from truly knowing?! Have you ever had an experience that you were sure of, only to find out that you were or should not have been so sure? Explain. Read Joshua 9 with special attention to verse 14 for a Scriptural example.

_____

_____

_____

These people in John 7 were sure about what they thought about the Messiah's origin but failed to remember Micah 5:2. When we think we don't know and even when we think we do know, it's always good to check with the One who DOES know via prayer and in His Word. When we look we must look with an open heart to receive His message and not the message we think we need to hear.

In John 7:38 Jesus uses the term living water. Living water is stated to well up into eternal life in John 4:14. In promising this Jesus is claiming to be God as that is a gift only God can give.

The people in this scene were too worried about what they thought they already knew to be teachable and they were too concerned about what others would think of them if they actually agreed and sided with Jesus.

How sad for us to gain the world and lose our soul. To trip over what we think rather than to be taught Truth, to sit because we are too afraid to stand for the One who stood for us on the cross.

Let's read Luke 9:26 as a warning. _____

We are still breathing for this moment. So this moment has been gifted to us to...

...continue standing for Him

...or maybe if need be, take the second chance to stand for and be taught by Him, with an open and circumcised heart that is willing to receive the rain as it comes and by His grace produce within it; to His glory.

Please record what has made the greatest impact on your heart today before closing.

_____

_____

_____

_____

Day 3: He Stood For YOU

Hi! I'm glad you're here. Please bow in prayer before embarking on todays journey. I'm praying to lay before Him an open heart to receive His hug, to receive His message that I might grow up further into Him. I'm also praying to lay aside all that I think I want to hear that He could come and bring what I should hear and it would be well received and applied in my life.

A treasure for the pocket of our hearts today: *For it is by grace you have been saved, through faith—and this is not from yourselves, it is a gift of God—* Ephesians 2:8 (NIV)

Please turn to John 7:53-8:11. _____

What do you notice between 7:53 and 8:1?

_____

Everyone went home but Jesus returned to the Mount of Olives.

Read Luke 9:58.

What might cause us to go home and leave Jesus outside under the trees?

_____

_____

It could be as simple as running to the grocery store for the big dinner you are planning for your friends and family only to become so wrapped up in your own list that you miss the tender expression of the elderly man behind you in the check out lane. As he watches your hustle and bustle he is reminded of his late wife that used to make everything so special too. However he now has no one to spend the holidays with. You check out, take your cart full without even looking up because if you get home soon enough… While the gentleman is left alone.

Dear God make us mindful of You in our gift of a day. *"The King will reply, 'Truly I tell you, whatever you did for one of the least of these brothers and sisters of mine, you did for me.'* Matthew 25:40 (NIV)

Do not forget to show hospitality to strangers, for by so doing some people have shown hospitality to angels without knowing it. Hebrews 13:2 (NIV)

Even though He was left out under the Olive Trees what is Jesus found doing in verse 2?

_____

He is not bitter about it but rather was up early and back at the Temple ready to teach the same people that left Him out in the cold the night before!!

Proverbs 8:17 promises us that if we seek Him we will find Him - no but's.

In John 8:3-4 what happens?

_____

According to Lev. 20:10 and Deut. 22:22 the law required that BOTH adulterous people, the woman AND the man, caught in the act were to be stoned. Clearly the religious leaders were not too concerned about THAT part of the law!

Have we ever distorted the Word to say what we want it to say when we want it to say it? It is of extreme importance to know the context of the Word making sure we do not use it inappropriately. What information do you gain from Exodus 20:7, Revelation 22:18-19, Deuteronomy 4:2 and John 7:18?

_____

_____

There is to be no altering of His Word what so ever, no taking it out of context.

Jesus stands ready to forgive any sin but confession and repentance must be followed by a true change of heart.

John 8:6 explains it plainly that these leaders were trying to trap Jesus. They kept pressing Jesus for an answer for if He said stone her they could report Him to the Romans who forbid the Jews to carry out their own executions (Jn. 18:31) and if He said not to stone her He would violate the law of Moses.

John 8:7 tells us they kept demanding an answer so what does Jesus do?

_____

He STANDS UP. In the circle of accusers He stands up for her. Not to condone her sin but to set her free from it!! (John 8:36)

John 8:9 (NLT) states, *When the accusers heard this, they slipped away one by one, beginning with the oldest, until only Jesus was left in the middle of the crowd with the woman.* (Verse 10) *Then Jesus stood up again...*

JESUS was left in the MIDDLE of the crowd STANDING UP for the sinner everyone else wanted to kill. What did He stand up from (verse 8)?

_____

Writing in the dust. I wonder if what He was writing in dust was a future so bright it stunned everyone including the women!

Isaiah 61:3 tells us He makes beauty from ashes. From but dust, He can create beauty dear one!
What does Jesus say to her in John 8:11?

_____

He gives her the gift of another moment to choose to stand for Him!!

Today will you boldly stand for Him who stood for you on the cross? Do you have a breath, a heartbeat in this moment? It's a gift, the time is now! May we receive the rain, the living water of His Spirit to help us to stand up for Him, back.

2 Corinthians 6:2 (NIV) *...I tell you, now is the time of God's favor, now is the day of salvation.*

If you have never prayed in your heart to receive Jesus as your personal Savior there is no time like the present. There is no magic prayer just in your heart confess your need for a Savior and that you believe Jesus is it. Tell Him you believe His death on the cross was in your place to pay for all your sins, past, present and future. Tell Him you believe He rose again conquering death, sin and the devil once and for all. Tell Him you want to give your life to Him and that you want Him living in you.

Because He lives we can too for eternity in Heaven. Oh dear one if you prayed to receive Jesus as your Savior today please tell another believer so that they can rejoice and encourage you in your faith! *I tell you that in the same way there will be more rejoicing in heaven over one sinner who repents than over ninety-nine righteous persons who do not need to repent.* Luke 15:7 (NIV)

Read: Romans 3:23, 6:23, 5:8, John 3:16, Romans 10:9-13, 8:1, 38-39, John 14:6

Please record the piece of greatest impact from today.

_____

_____

_____

_____

Day 4: A Great Treasure

Hello, I'm so glad you are here! I might say that every time but I truly am thankful for the motivation, the expectation of your fellowship alongside me in the Word, brings to me. I was reminded just this morning in Galatians 2:20 NLT that it is only through trust that I will fulfill God's great plan for my life. ...*So I live in this earthly body by trusting in the Son of God, who loved me and gave himself for me.* The more I study just who He is, the more intimate my relationship with Him becomes as I discover more of His lovingly faithful and trustworthy character thus emboldening my trust in Him. I hope and pray that this study has emboldened your faith as it has mine as we have dug so deeply into His heart via His Word together. Let's keep at it with some hupomone! (That's Greek for patient endurance.)

But the one who endures to the end will be saved. Matthew 24:13 (ESV) Let's tuck this into our heart's pocket as we begin again today to know Him more deeply.

After opening in prayer please meet me on the other side of John 8:12-30.

———

Oh how encouraging the first sentence is! What does Jesus declare to be?
I Am …

———————————————————

Jesus uses His name declared in Exodus 3:14 "I AM", here in John 8:12 and reveals more of Himself in that I AM (He) is the Light of the world! Psalm 36:9 tells us, *For with you is the fountain of life; in your light we see light.*
What does John 8:12 promise us if we walk in His Light?

———————————————————

We won't walk in darkness. What does it feel like to walk in darkness? Remember back to the last time you were stumbling around in the dark for something (quite possibly the light switch) and describe your emotional state. Or maybe your emotional state after stepping on the LEGO in the dark and then walking into the drawer that was left open right at shin level!

———————————————————

Walking in the dark or the effects of walking in the dark are never pleasant.

Walking in the Light of Jesus we don't have to feel that way! We may not understand or see our way but we know THE WAY, The Master Planner, The One who promises to make our path straight and all things to work together and to get us safely to the Kingdom if we will just trust Him, submit our will to Him. God Almighty must lead dear one if we are to walk in His Light of true and abundant life. Too often I rob myself of His true Light and life because I unpack my little flashlight thinking "I got this God, don't worry it's

LED I'll be fine!" WRONG! What is my little pocket LED flashlight compared to the Light of the world!?!!

Often the geese fly overhead in the shape of a V and it always reminds me of John 14:6. Please write it out below.

_____

_____

Jesus is the Way. If He showed those geese the way to fly in a V which is the shape of an arrow across the sky (such a miracle) then I'm going to take each V flight of geese I see over my head as a love note from God. His note to my heart reminding me He too will show me the way in my life as I choose to follow, trusting Him to teach me and guide me and lead me as His Word promises.

I will instruct you and teach you in the way you should go; I will counsel you with my loving eye on you. Psalm 32:8 (NIV)

Why did the Pharisees feel Jesus' claim was invalid?

_____

Deuteronomy 19:15 tells us by law there needed to be at least two witnesses to a claim. Between Jesus and the Father who sent Him that law was fulfilled however because the Pharisees were unfamiliar with Jesus' true origin they failed to see the validity and life saving Truth being held out to them.

What type of search is described in...
Jeremiah 29:13
Deuteronomy 4:29

_____

These verses do not describe a half hearted search but a very diligent seeking with all heart and soul!!

Can you remember a time you sought something with such urgency?

_____

_____

The Pharisees missed an important truth because they had closed the door before openly and honestly searching Him out. Let's learn from the mistakes outlined in Scripture rather than repeat them.

In John 8:23 Jesus tells them they belong to this world and He does not. It is only by believing in the One who penetrated our dark world with His Light of salvation that we can be saved. Are we looking for answers in life in places other than in the Light of Jesus? Let's be careful not to get wrapped up in the world's value system (achievements, appearances, approval of men...) that we miss what is of true value which is life in the Light of Christ. Psalm 27:1 (ESV) *The LORD is my light and my salvation; whom shall I fear? The LORD is the stronghold of my life; of whom shall I be afraid?*

Of all the strongholds the world tries to shove in our direction that only end in chains may we in His wisdom always choose Jesus alone to be the Stronghold of Truth and Light that we cling to and that sets us free!

John 8:20 (NLT) *Jesus made these statements while he was teaching in the section of the Temple known as the Treasury. But he was not arrested, because his time had not yet come.*

What section of the Temple was Jesus speaking in?

_____

This section was located in the Court of Women. Jesus often taught in this section of the Temple so that both men AND women could listen to His teaching. Jesus elevated the importance of women as human beings alongside men in His attention and care of them and willingness to involve them in His ministry.

He loves you dear one, you are not "less than" but rather His GREAT treasure!! No matter where you have been or what you have done or what's been done to you, you are wanted and valued in God's eyes as His precious creation! He stood for your honor at the cross as He gave His life for yours that you might choose to live in the purifying Light of His Truth and be set free!

Do you trust the One who created sight and things to be seen to be your eyes when you can't see? Do you trust the one who created ears and sound to hear when you can't? Remember your weakness will never be too strong for His strength. It's only when we are willing to trust, that He can take us to the heights He's planned for our treasured life in Him.

Yet you, LORD, are our Father. We are the clay, you are the potter; we are all the work of your hand. Isaiah 64:8 (NIV) *So in Christ Jesus you are all children of God through faith,* Galatians 3:26 (NIV) *But we have this treasure in jars of clay to show that this all-surpassing power is from God and not from us.* 2 Corinthians 4:7 (NIV)

Please record what has made the most impact on your heart today.

_____

_____

_____

_____

Day 5: Our Good Father God

What better way to close out a week than in His Word right! Thank you for meeting me here once again. Please grab God's hand and begin in prayer.

The Spirit you received does not make you slaves, so that you live in fear again; rather, the Spirit you received brought about your adoption to sonship. And by him we cry, "Abba,

Father." Romans 8:15 (NIV) Let us tuck that in our heart's pocket as we start dear one.

Please read now John 8:31-59. _____

According to verse 31 what is the key to knowing Truth and being set free?

_____

Remaining faithful to His teachings.

What does remaining faithful to His teachings look like to you?

_____

_____

_____

John 14:6 tells us Jesus IS Truth. Knowing Him brings discernment between right and wrong and to choose right in Him sets us free from the sin that so easily entangles us. What advice does Hebrews 12:1 give us in this area?

_____

_____

Throw off all sin! Sin only keeps you from fulfilling God's GREAT plan for your life and becoming all that He dreamed up in you!

What is the main point of argument concerning fathers in our John passage today?

_____

_____

John 8:37-38 (NLT) states, ...*And yet some of you are trying to kill me because there's no room in your hearts for my message. I am telling you what I saw when I was with my Father. But you are following the advice of your father."*

Please circle the "f" in both of the words "father". You circled the same letter but what was different about them?

_____

One was a capital letter and one was a lower case letter. How often do we construct our capital "F" Father into a lower case "f" father? Lower case "f" father's are human fathers and susceptible to imperfections as we all are but our Heavenly (capital "F") Father is perfect always and when we "make no room in our hearts" for His message we have overstepped our bounds and have now become bound by Satan's schemes!

Satan was using the Pharisees bitterness, pride and prejudices to keep their hearts hard and minds closed to Truth. What tools do we readily hand the enemy to use against us?
Isaiah 54:17 tells us NO weapon FORMED against us will prevail. So if we stand in Him victorious, why oh why do we choose to quench His Spirit and hand the enemy tools like our own lack of forgiveness, foolish pride, selfish ambition and vain conceit to use against us?!

As the arguments over who Jesus is heats up in John chapter 8 what does Jesus say Abraham did in verse 56?

_____

Abraham saw the promise through faith. All the world is blessed through Jesus! (See Genesis 12:1-7; 15:1-21; Hebrews 11:8-19)

What was the people's complaint in John 8:57 and how does Jesus respond in verse 58?

_____

_____

This is powerful! Jesus states He existed before Abraham and He uses God's holy name as stated in Exodus 3:14! He is proclaiming to be God and this demands a response from every heart.

How are you holding out that claim of Truth for others to respond to in the way you live your life?

_____

_____

Therefore, since we have such a hope, we are very bold. 2 Corinthians 3:12 (NIV)
making the most of every opportunity, because the days are evil. Ephesians 5:16 (NIV)

You, dear children, are from God and have overcome them, because the one who is in you is greater than the one who is in the world. 1 John 4:4 (NIV)

Take hold of and share His Truth that you are His treasure and He is yours, beyond compare!

John 8:59 (NLT) states, *At that point they picked up stones to throw at him. But Jesus was hidden from them and left the Temple.*

Even Jesus faced hardship in sharing the Truth so we can expect the same, but that second sentence says in the enemies attacks Jesus was hidden from them… Please read Psalm 91 as we close and especially savor verse 4 NLT, *He will cover you with his feathers. He will shelter you with his wings. His faithful promises are your armor and protection.* Oh dear one He is just too great a treasure to miss!

May He be the treasured Light in your heart, the Truth in your mind and the Way of your Life's steps as you tuck up under His wing treasured close to His heart.

Please record what made the most impact on you today as you studied.

_____

_____

_____

_____

Day 6 & 7: At His Feet - A Time to Reflect

Over the next two days take time to reflect over your week of study. Maybe you need some time to catch up on the study material and this might be the perfect break to do just that with the Lord!

I encourage you to glance back at the final point at the end of each day that you recorded having had the greatest impact on your heart. As you spend time with God in prayer, reflect and record on the lines below how God is tying it all together and applying it to your life.

Ask that God make it clear who He would have you invite into a natural opportunity to share Him, to apply what you are learning. Trust Him to continue to take the lead. May we have a heart ever ready with eyes and ears out to the opportunities God wants to invite us into for His glory and praise.

Do not merely listen to the word, and so deceive yourselves. Do what it says. Anyone who listens to the word but does not do what it says is like someone who looks at his face in a mirror and, after looking at himself, goes away and immediately forgets what he looks like. But whoever looks intently into the perfect law that gives freedom, and continues in it - not forgetting what they have heard, but doing it - they will be blessed in what they do.
James 1:22-25 (NIV)

_____

_____

_____

Philippians 4:13 (NIV) *I can do all things through him who gives me strength.*

John 14:26 (NIV) *But the Advocate, the Holy Spirit, whom the Father will send in my name, will teach you all things and will remind you of everything I have said to you.*

WEEK 10

The thief comes only to steal and kill and destroy; I have come that they may have life, and have it to the full. John 10:10 (NIV)

Day 1: TRUST

My goodness gracious! Here we are, by His goodness and grace, at the end of our 10 week study! Well, almost anyway! Over the next four days we will be going off the beaten path just a bit. If you have been traveling with me since "TRUST in The Light", you may recall we ended that book with a glimpse into the life of a dear gal named Rahab. When we closed that study book we were all raising our stone of remembrance, our Ebenezer, with the word "TRUST" written across it. Today we will circle back to our foundation stone, our Rock as we seek to build our lives upon it/Him, that we might truly LIVE! Without further delay let us bow and pray.

I keep my eyes always on the LORD. With him at my right hand, I will not be shaken. Psalm 16:8 (NIV)

In day 2, week 1 of "TRUST in the Light" we read through the genealogy of Jesus in Matthew 1:1-17_____. Please begin in that passage of Scripture and again list below the only four women included in the list (with the exception of Mary, the mother of Jesus).

1.) _____

2.) _____

3.) _____

4.) _____

*Verse 3: Tamar: slept with her father in law / Verse 5: Rahab: a woman in the business of prostitution / Verse 5: Ruth: a pagan gal / Verse 6: Bathsheba: committed adultery

God wanted, loved and transformed with Truth what most of the world would have thrown away. I asked this question before but it bares asking again… Are we allowing that very same God to work that very same transforming Truth into and over our own lives?

_____

Please read the definition of love as God defines it in 1 Corinthians 13: 4-8 _____.

Please list the 7 things that God says love IS.

1.) _____

2.) _____

3.) _____

4.) _____

5.) _____

6.) _____

7.) _____

Please list the 9 things that God says love is NOT.

1.) _____

2.) _____

3.) _____

4.) _____

5.) _____

6.) _____

7.) _____

8.) _____

9.) _____

It would seem love is not driven or directed by feelings. It is as I've heard it stated, feelings are not facts. Please fill in the blanks below according to Romans 5:8 (NIV) to see how God Almighty expressed His love for us.

But God demonstrates his own _____ for us in this: _____ we were _____ sinners, Christ _____ for us.
(love, while, still, died)

What part of Jesus do you think FELT like dying for sinners?!

Please visit with me Matthew 26:36-46. _____

How many times did Jesus pray for another way to save us? _____
Three times Jesus asked the Father if there might be another way for us to enter salvation. But no, there was not, and Jesus submitted and received the "no" for our better "yes". He went to hell to defeat death, the devil and all the powers sin might have over us once and for all of time, rising victorious so that we could too! We don't have to stay down, we can rise each time we fall, because He did.

Micah 7:8 (NIV) Do not gloat over me, my enemy! Though I have fallen, I will rise. Though I sit in darkness, the LORD will be my light. Proverbs 24:16 (NIV) for though the righteous fall seven times, they rise again, but the wicked stumble when calamity strikes. John 14:6 (NIV) Jesus answered, "I am the way and the truth and the life. No one comes to the Father except through me.

Matthew 26:38 records Jesus saying His soul is overwhelmed with sorrow to the point of death. I don't know your story but maybe you have been in a place in which you felt/feel your soul overwhelmed with sorrow, even to the point of death.

Dear one, Jesus truly understands and He took the cross so your life would not have to end in that state.

What is the one thing Jesus repeatedly encourages His disciples to pray for in our Matthew passage?

_____

For the strength to withstand falling to temptation. The enemy of our souls is quick to pounce when we are down feeding into all the lies. Jesus urged His men to PRAY! Praying is like holding God's hand and there is none stronger than Him to steady us, to speak foundational Truth we can stand up on in our time of need. Psalm 34:18 (NIV) *The Lord is close to the broken hearted and saves those who are crushed in spirit.* Isaiah 41:13 (NIV) *For I am the Lord your God who takes hold of your right and and says to you, Do not fear; I will help you.*

Before we head to our last portion of Scripture for today please glance back at 1 Corinthians 13:8-13. _____

Verse 12 tells us we are not going to know and understand it all this side of heaven but do not give up in what we cannot comprehend yet! One day we shall know! How will we know? Verse 12 tells us even as "I AM FULLY KNOWN" (emphasis mine) Does that touch your heart like it does mine?! To know in all that you don't know, YOU are FULLY known!!

The One who knit your heart together sees it and understands and loves you completely! There is nothing missed or misunderstood. The good the bad the beautiful and the ugly...you are KNOWN **and** LOVED.

Take a look with me at Ephesians 1:7-8. _____

What do we have as believers in Jesus?

_____

_____

Redemption through his blood and the forgiveness of sin (there is nothing His blood does not cover - fully) by His amazing grace that He LAVISHED on us!! Completely undeserved and what gets me is in verse 8, He did all this with ALL wisdom and understanding! He knew me FULLY (all my flaws, failures and faults) and still, still He chose to die for me - for you - that He might redeem life from the pit of hell that we deserved and bring us rather to be with Him in Paradise for eternity!!! AMAZING GRACE!

On the cross Jesus said, "It is finished." (John 19:30) He did ALL the work, dear one. Salvation is by grace through faith. (Ephesians 2:8) Believe in Jesus and be saved. (John 3:16) We can't make ourselves worthy, we can't be good enough, we all fell short and needed a Savior - Jesus is it. Receive the free gift and live.

In closing please meet me on the other side of Ephesians 2:1-10. _____

Verse 4 (NIV): *But because of his great love for us, God, who is rich in mercy, made us alive with Christ even when we were dead in transgressions - it is by grace you have been saved.*

Our God we can trust. His love is unmatched. As we proceed through our week of study let's build upon Who we know is Faithful and True. (Rev. 19:11)

For no one can lay any foundation other than the one already laid, which is Jesus Christ. 1 Corinthians 3:11 (NIV) Upon Him, I lay my trust.

Please recored that which had the most impact on your heart today.

_____

_____

_____

_____

Day 2: Out Of Control

Welcome my friend. Today we have some ground to cover and a new friend to meet in Scripture so let's begin right away in prayer. I'm praying to follow God's lead through His Word today and that we receive God's perspective and message as we study.

Let's tuck this treasure in our hearts pocket as we pray it's Truth take root in our lives. Isaiah 50:4 (NIV) *The Sovereign LORD has given me a well-instructed tongue, to know the word that sustains the weary. He wakens me morning by morning, wakens my ear to listen like one being instructed.*

Please take your time as you read through 2 Samuel 11. _____

List the scandals, the brokenness in just this one chapter.

_____

_____

Murder, affair, deception, … This chapter finishes in verse 27 telling us that Bathsheba gave birth to her and David's child, a son, yet the thing David had done displeased the Lord.

Deuteronomy 29:29 (NIV) *The secret things belong to the LORD our God, but the things revealed belong to us and to our children forever...* We do not hear Bathsheba speak up much in this chapter other than that she mourned her husband, Uriah's death. We can surmise many things but it's best to just stick to what has been revealed to us.

Sometimes the heartache that happens to us in this broken world is out of our control and sometimes it's due to our own misuse of control. Either way we can rejoice that God has told us He has overcome the brokenness of this world by the cross! John 16:33 (NIV) *"I have told you these things, so that in me you may have peace. In this world you will have trouble. But take heart! I have overcome the world."*

Please read further into this story now in 2 Samuel 12:1-25. _____

This, no doubt, is a very difficult passage to digest and not one we will be able to fully, in just the next page or so of this study. I believe many of the questions this passage may stir up are ones to save for when we see God in heaven.

This side of heaven we are faced with many questions that I believe have answers beyond our comprehension at this time. I believe that is why He alone can offer a peace unlike this world can offer and that surpasses comprehension as we choose to trust His faithful promises. We must measure our circumstances by His love displayed on the cross and not His love by our circumstances still beyond our comprehension.

What strikes me the most, and I believe those in the passage as well, is verse 20. What does David do in verse 20 that perplexes everyone around?

The heartache Bathsheba and David were experiencing I believe is of the worst kind. They were faced with the unthinkable. Yet after the fact in verse 20 David get's up and worships! How is that possible when you have been through a tragedy that takes all reason to continue breathing seemingly away?!

I cling to verse 2 Samuel 12:23.

(NIV) *But now that he is dead, why should I go on fasting? Can I bring him back again? I will go to him, but he will not return to me."*

God alone gives breath and if you still have one it's because He still believes He can bring glory to His name through your life. There are plans, purpose and power for those willing to get up and receive it. We all have one life to live this side of heaven and before we even came to be our days were numbered. (Job 14:5) No tragedy has the power to cut short or change them. God hates death and it was never His plan. John 11 records Jesus' heartbreak over it and yet in that same chapter He declares Himself to be the resurrection and the life! John 11:25 (NIV) *Jesus said to her, "I am the resurrection and the life. The one who believes in me will live, even though they die; and whoever lives by believing in me will never die. Do you believe this?"*

Do you believe this?

I believe David and Bathsheba did. 2 Samuel 12:23 tells us David said, he would go to his son one day not the other way around. If we are honest, anyone we know that has gone to heaven before us, if given a choice would rather wait it out there for us to join them rather than return here to earth!

There are consequences for sin and sometimes we unfortunately are on the receiving end of someone else's sin. This world is broken but Jesus allowed

Himself to be broken so that we could be made whole - every single one of us.

Praise God He is in control and we arrive in eternity safely (2 Timothy 4:18) but we must choose to LIVE the moments we have until we get there. Jesus died that we might LIVE and not under the rock of regret or in the shadow of shame or in constant tears of tragedy but truly live with Hope. Hope in the Resurrection and the Life! God Almighty, the only One who controls the breath that makes your chest rise and fall gives you just that (your breath) as evidence that He isn't finished with you yet. When all feels out of control trust the One who remains, at all times, in control.

Psalm 16:8 (NIV) *I keep my eyes always on the LORD. With him at my right hand, I will not be shaken.*

Please do not finish without soaking in the Living Hope of 1 Corinthians 15:55-57 dear one. _____

Please record what impacted your heart the most from your study today.

_____

_____

_____

_____

1 Peter 1:3 (NIV) *Praise be to the God and Father of our Lord Jesus Christ! In his great mercy he has given us new birth into a living hope through the resurrection of Jesus Christ from the dead,*

Day 3: Faith Faces Forward

Welcome, I'm so very glad you are here. I'm incredibly grateful for the encouragement your life has brought me as we have studied His Word together. Just the idea of you on the other side of this page… that I am not alone on this quest toward our eternal Home has spurred my heart onward! Romans 1:12 (NIV) *that is, that you and I may be mutually encouraged by each other's faith.*

As you pray to our Heavenly Father before embarking further, please also let the prayer in Ephesians 3:14-21 wash over you. _____

Please glance back at the chapter of Scripture we studied yesterday. What occurs in 2 Samuel 12:24-25?

_____

David and Bathsheba have another son they name Solomon.

Verse 24 states that the Lord loved this child and because He did, He sent word through the prophet Nathan to call him what (verse 25)?

_____

There is no human being God creates that He does not love! He may not love our actions at times but He loves those He has made in His image (Gen. 1:27).

God loved David and Bathsheba's first son just as much as He loved their second. The purpose of each life is the same in that we are to reflect His glory, the glory of our Creator however the angle to which we reflect Him all hangs a bit differently in terms of time and place. We are all God alone's, bright idea. As much as we would like to try and control the way and outcome of not only our own lives but of those we love we must remember even our best ideas on our best days all pale in comparison to the great and almighty perfect plans of our Savior for not only us but for those we hold dear as well.

Jeremiah 29:11 (NIV) *For I know the plans I have for you," declares the Lord, "plans to prosper you and not to harm you, plans to give you a hope and a future.*

Nowhere in that verse does it say the PROCESS would be fun, easy or understandable or even that it would align with our preconceived expectations! When was the last time losing weight was a fun process?! The end result is AMAZING… the process… not so much. We must trust the promise if we are going to live the life He purposed, allowing others to live out theirs too in Him. This takes me back to the name God sent word through Nathan to give David and Bathsheba concerning their second son.

The end of 2 Samuel 12:24 records that God loved that baby boy. He also loved David and Bathsheba and probably knew about their heightened concern for the little ones life considering what happened before. I wonder if David and Bathsheba had lingering concern that the sin of their past might not have been fully forgiven?! I believe God wanted David and Bathsheba to rest in His forgiveness and enjoy His love not only for them but also over this new blessing. Jedidiah means loved by the Lord. Again God loved their first baby just as much, and his little life was purposeful and powerful and accomplished all that God desired. That little one in a short amount of time turned eyes and hearts (for all of time) up to God. That is the greatest thing any of us could hope to accomplish in life.

Before moving into young Solomon's life please read the following verses and record below the impact they make to your heart.
Psalm 103:12

Psalm 51:7

_____

Micah 7:19

_____

Hebrews 8:12

_____

Hebrews 10:22

_____

Hebrews 9:14

_____

Hebrews 9:14 tells us even our conscience is cleansed!! Why, so that we can serve the living God! Remarkable! If that doesn't silence all the lies of the enemy in your head that there, in Truth, is purpose and life beyond failure in Jesus! You are wanted and loved beyond your mistakes and you are not defined by your failures but rather by His display of ultimate love as He gave His life on the cross so that you and I could walk free from the chains of sin, death and the devil in order that we might LIVE!! LIVE in great purpose, power and plans that far exceed our own! Faith faces one direction and that is forward. I pray you are walking forward and free dear one.

Before we close today please read 1 Kings 3:1-17. _____

Out of murder, affairs, deception, and heartache of the deepest kind, God as only He can, brought beauty from ashes. When God redeems none can compare! Solomon, David and Bathsheba's son, arose as the wisest king to ever live through which God used to write some of the book of Proverbs, the book of wisdom for us all! The book of wisdom, of wise advice! Who would have thought?! ...God did! Out of our most moronic mistakes can be birthed the wisest of miracles! Only in Jesus! Praise Him, Oh Praise Him!!

Please record the point of greatest impact on your heart today.

_____

_____

_____

_____

Day 4: Raise Your Ebenezer

Well done, WELL done my friend! Here we are by God's grace at the end of an in-depth study of His Word. I pray as we close this book we open a new chapter in our walk of faith with our God! LIVING like we KNOW whom we believe, LIVING like we are convinced He is able, able to guard what we have entrusted to Him until the day of His return! (2 Timothy 1:12) Dear one, we must LIVE entrusted.

Please begin in prayer that God Almighty lead us through a strong finish.

Please tuck one more treasured Truth into that pocket in your heart. John 10:10 (NIV) *The thief comes only to steal and kill and destroy; I have come that they may have life, and have it to the full.*

Please begin in 1 Samuel 7. _____

In verses 2-3 there was a turning from sin and toward the Lord. What were they asked to do in verse 3 to show their hearts were genuine?

_____

They needed to rid themselves of all the foreign gods. We can't run forward in the race of faith God has marked out for us if we are all tangled up in sin!

Read Hebrews 12:1-3. _____
*Throw off sin.

*Run with perseverance.

*Fix your eyes on the One who persevered for you... so that you won't lose heart.

In 1 Samuel 7:5 and in verse 8 Samuel is crying out to the Lord and encouraged to keep it up! What does 1 Thessalonians 5:17 advise us to do?

_____

Pray without ceasing. Prayer is like holding God's hand and it is only in His strength that we will remain steadfast and firm in our faith to the finish.

Upon victory what does Samuel do in 1 Samuel 7:12?

_____

_____

He set up a stone, a memorial of sorts, naming it Ebenezer or stone of help Declaring, *"Thus far the LORD has helped us." (NIV)*

May we never forget where our help comes from.

David and Bathsheba did not forget. As Samuel set up a stone of remembrance we will see David and Bathsheba set up, or encourage, their son Solomon to remember where not only his help would come from but from where theirs came from.

Glance first at 1 Chronicles 29:19 and record below David's prayer for his young son, Solomon.

_____

_____

As you pray this for yourself who else do you pray this over?

_____

Glance over now at 1 Chronicles 28:20 and record what advice David gives to his son, Solomon.

_____

_____

David had a faith that had been strengthened in the fire of trial. The enemy purposes our fiery trials to consume us, so when we choose not to fall away from the faith on account of what God allows (Matthew 11:6, Romans 8:28) we emerge refined with a strength of faith that will encourage everyone around us (Job 23:10, 1 Peter 1:7)!

Blessed is anyone who does not stumble on account of me." Matthew 11:6 (NIV)

in order that Satan might not outwit us. For we are not unaware of his schemes. 2 Corinthians 2:11 (NIV)

Yesterday we touched on one of the author's God used to write Proverbs, known as the book of wisdom in the Bible. What was his name again?

_____

Solomon.

Now please flip all the way to the last chapter of Proverbs. Please read Proverbs 31. _____

This seems to be advice from a queen mother to her son. Although probably not written by Bathsheba I believe her heart could have spoken similarly. Wisdom is often birthed via experience and those who are wise will heed wise instruction.

David and Bathsheba had not only been involved in the unthinkable they had experienced it. But... they got up again, they continued breathing and by the redeeming grace of God they LIVED out what was still great purpose in His power.

Solomon needed their reflection of His glory.
Someone needs your reflection of His glory.

Be on your guard; stand firm in the faith; be courageous; be strong. 1 Corinthians 16:13 (NIV)

Bathsheba experienced unthinkable tragedies on multiple levels and emerged not bitter but better - only by His grace.

She chose not to give up but to allow His Spirit, the breath of the Almighty to fill up her lungs and keep breathing. *The Spirit of God has made me; the breath of the Almighty gives me life.* Job 33:4 (NIV)
She chose not to give up but to look up, allowing Him to be the lifter of her head. *But you, LORD, are a shield around me, my glory, the One who lifts my head high.* Psalm 3:3 (NIV)

She chose not to give up but to take His outstretched hand and get up, for "Thus far the Lord had helped her. *For I am the LORD your God who takes hold of your right hand and says to you, Do not fear; I will help you.* Isaiah 41:13 (NIV)

TRUST Him, someone needs the reflection of His glory through your life.

Before you tuck this book back on the shelf, I encourage you to find one small rock to symbolize a steppingstone of faith, a steppingstone of remembrance. Write the word "LIVE" on it and place it where it will stand as a reminder to you of all that God has taught you these past 10 weeks. (If you completed

"TRUST in The Light" maybe place it next to your "TRUST" rock.) He is Faithful and True, a solid foundation upon which you can place your trust and LIVE abundantly, unshaken.

Today, choose to raise your Ebenezer and LIVE in the Light! *"For thus far the LORD has helped us."* (1 Sam. 7:12 NIV)

For you were once darkness, but now you are light in the Lord. Live as children of light Ephesians 5:8 (NIV) *The LORD is my light and my salvation; whom shall I fear? The LORD is the stronghold of my life; of whom shall I be afraid?* Psalm 27:1 (ESV) *For you have delivered me from death and my feet from stumbling, that I may walk before God in the light of life.* Psalm 56:13 (NIV)

Thank you most sincerely and may God bless you muchly dear one~ Janette

Day 5: At His Feet - A Time to Reflect

Today reflect over this final week of study. (During days 6 and 7 of study this week you will have a chance to circle back and reflect over the ENTIRE study with God.) I encourage you to spend time in prayer now and record on the lines below how God is tying it together and applying this past weeks study to your life specifically for such a time as this.

Ask that God make it clear who He would have you invite into a natural opportunity to share Him, to apply what you are learning. Trust Him to continue to take the lead. May we have a heart ever ready with eyes and ears out to the opportunities God wants to invite us into for His glory and praise.

Do not merely listen to the word, and so deceive yourselves. Do what it says. Anyone who listens to the word but does not do what it says is like someone who looks at his face in a mirror and, after looking at himself, goes away and immediately forgets what he looks like. But whoever looks intently into the perfect law that gives freedom, and continues in it - not forgetting what they have heard, but doing it - they will be blessed in what they do.
James 1:22-25 (NIV)

_____

_____

_____

_____

_____

_____

_____

_____

_____

Philippians 4:13 (NIV) *I can do all things through him who gives me strength.*
John 14:26 (NIV) *But the Advocate, the Holy Spirit, whom the Father will send in my name, will teach you all things and will remind you of everything I have said to you.*

Day 6 & 7: At His Feet – A Time to Reflect

Over the next two days take time to review each of your completed reflection sheets on each weeks days 6 and 7 along with your group study note page. As you lay it all at His feet, praise Him for the way He has faithfully led us through. Thank Him for revealing great and unsearchable things we did not know before we began. Ask that He continue to cultivate a craving for more of Him in our hearts and minds every day. Ask that we submit to a full invasion of Him within us that we might more clearly magnify His Light to this world for His glory and praise. Record below a summary of all your most impactful points gathered from each week and ask that God imprint His trustworthiness with His very own fingerprint on your heart.

_____

_____

_____

_____

_____

_____

_____

_____

_____

_____

_____

_____

_____

_____

_____

_____

Thank you muchly~ Janette

P.S. I truly hope you will join me for the third leg of our journey through the life of Jesus in, "REST in The Light" book 3 in the L.I.G.H.T. series.

To him who is able to keep you from stumbling and to present you before his glorious presence without fault and with great joy — to the only God our Savior be glory, majesty, power and authority, through Jesus Christ our Lord, before all ages, now and forevermore! Amen. Jude 1:24-25 (NIV)

STUDY GROUP DISCUSSION NOTE SPACE: Weeks 1-10

ABOUT: Redeeming grace 99|1 Ministries

Redeeming Grace 99|1 Ministries is based on Matthew 18:12-14. There is no situation, circumstance or life God cannot reach, restore, revive and fully redeem for our good and His glory. Redeeming grace is the criminal on the cross entering into Paradise; it's Ruth the pagan becoming part of Jesus' genealogy; it's Jairus' daughter brought back to life; it's Joseph pulled from the prison and made a mighty leader; it's Daniel on the other side of the lion's den; it's Saul turned Paul; it's Jonah out of the whale; it's David and Bathsheba's son Solomon; it's Hannah having Samuel after barrenness; it's the man lame for 38 years made to walk; it's five loaves and two fish becoming a meal feeding 5,000 with leftovers; it's Lazarus walking out of the tomb; it's the widow's oil that never ran out; it's the parting of the Red Sea and the receding of the Jordan; it's you and I realizing our need for a Savior as we look to Jesus high and lifted up, believing His death on the cross was in our place for our sin, then resurrecting from the grave God defeating the enemy of our souls once and for all. We are made new in receiving the transforming Truth of His love so that we might be made a vessel of His victory. His redeeming grace writes living hope on every page of our lives. You have never laid eyes on someone God did not love. Our mission is to reach one, and then another and another…with the Good News of His redeeming grace for us all through Jesus, raising the population of heaven by His grace, to His glory and praise.

Redeeming Grace 99|1 Ministries graphic designs © 2020
Design credit: Noah Kieffer

ABOUT THE AUTHOR

By God's amazing grace, Janette resides in Colorado with her husband (married in 2003) their six children and lovable dog named Brave. As a teacher by trade, she finds joy in learning and sharing her passion for the hope filled Word of God.

Find other books by Janette Kieffer on Amazon such as…

"Reigning in the Rain" is a one year devotional study journal that will encourage you to see Living Hope on every page of your life.

"TRUST in The Light" is book one in a 4 part series. This series studies the life of Jesus through the harmony of the four gospels. Go back to what you know to find your faith in all that you do not. Allow God to use your questions, doubts, fears, failures, even your triumphs as tools to bring Truth into the Light. Truth you never would have known otherwise. With the rock of ever-increasing TRUST lay the first steppingstone of your faith on the firm foundation of the Faithful and True. He is the same yesterday, today and forever. In an ever-changing world come delight yourself in the Light of God's love for you that will not falter, fail or fade. TRUST in the Light.

May the God of hope fill you with all joy and peace as you trust in him, so that you may overflow with hope by the power of the Holy Spirit. Romans 15:13 (NIV)

Made in the USA
Middletown, DE
07 January 2023

20745377R00113